Customers for Life

"So often when we read business books two thoughts cross our minds: 1) 'I wonder if the author follows his own teachings?' and 2) 'If the author is so smart, why isn't he rich?'

"Well, in Carl Sewell's case, the 250-million-dollar business he built answers both questions. *Customers for Life* is a gold mine of good ideas . . . with a nugget on every page."

—Stew Leonard, owner, Stew Leonard's Dairy

CUSTOMERS FOR LIFE

How to Turn That One-Time Buyer into a Lifetime Customer

by CARL SEWELL
and PAUL B. BROWN

NEW YORK   LONDON   TORONTO   SYDNEY   AUCKLAND

A CURRENCY BOOK
PUBLISHED BY DOUBLEDAY
a division of Bantam Doubleday Dell Publishing Group, Inc.
666 Fifth Avenue, New York, New York 10103

CURRENCY and DOUBLEDAY
are trademarks of Doubleday, a division of
Bantam Doubleday Dell Publishing Group, Inc.

PRINTING HISTORY:
First printing: August 24, 1990
Second printing: October 22, 1990
Third printing: November 5, 1990
Fourth printing: November 13, 1990
Fifth printing: November 21, 1990
Sixth printing: December 18, 1990
Seventh printing: January 25, 1991
Eighth printing: March 15, 1991
Ninth printing: April 5, 1991
Tenth printing: May 24, 1991
Eleventh printing: September 18, 1991
Twelfth printing: October 21, 1991

LIBRARY OF CONGRESS CATALOGING-IN-PUBLICATION DATA
Sewell, Carl.
    Customers for life : how to turn that one-time buyer into a
    lifetime customer / by Carl Sewell and Paul B. Brown.—1st ed.
       p.   cm.
    "A Currency book"—T.p. verso.
    1. Customer service.   2. Automobile industry and trade—
Customer service—United States.   3. Automobile dealers—
United States.
I. Brown, Paul B.   II. Title.
HF5415.5.S49   1990
658.'8'12—dc20
ISBN 0-385-41503-6

While it goes without saying that this is for Peggy, Jacquelin, and Carl, it's dedicated to Erik Jonsson, Stanley Marcus, Bob Moore, John Sewell, and my father.

And to Shannon Rachel Peck Brown, because it's her turn.

Contents

Foreword
by Tom Peters

This exceptional book has one entire section—four full chapters—on asking the customer exactly what he or she wants. Another entire chapter is devoted to restrooms—the proper appointments and their impact on customer perceptions. Yet another chapter dwells exclusively on signage.

This from a man who has expanded his business from $10 million in 1968 to $250 million today, with accompanying profit growth of the same magnitude. Carl Sewell sells cars—Cadillacs and Hyundais, Lexuses and Chevrolets. His customer satisfaction scores are the auto-industry equivalent of a 3-minute, 30-second mile. He doesn't merely top the charts, he keeps redefining "best."

At times this stunning book is homely: don't charge customers for any service you wouldn't charge a friend for. (That means sending a service technician—they're on call twenty-four hours a day, seven days a week—out to the Dallas airport at midnight to replace a broken key in a customer's ignition, for free.) Ethics: Guide your business by asking, "How would this action look as a page 1 news story in tomorrow morning's paper?"

At times it amazes: Sewell believes in psychological testing for would-be employees. Yet his ultimate hiring test: do they fidget during interviews? He likes energetic folks. If you *can* sit still for an interview, you're not his cup of tea.

Carl Sewell has been setting standards for auto dealer service (an oxymoron?) for years. It started with opening the service department Saturdays and providing a few "loaner cars" for customers to use while theirs was being serviced. Now his Cadillac dealer loaner car fleet alone numbers 150 (there are loaners at his Hyundai operation, too). But he's hardly rested on his laurels: the Cadillac and Lexus operations recently hired assistants for each salesperson—they deliver loaners to the customers' homes and pick up the cars to be repaired or tuned up.

Sewell bought a street sweeper to keep the roads clean in front of the dealership, since he didn't think the city's service was up to snuff (and first impressions, he counsels, are all-important and all too often ignored). Then there's the restaurant, Celebration, that he has cajoled into opening a branch in one of his dealerships—to occupy customers who've decided to wait out the car-repair process.

These are wonderful stories that add up to a heartening message about the possibilities and payoffs from matchless customer service. Moreover, the approach has proven as applicable for his Hyundai and Chevrolet dealerships as for Cadillac and Lexus. I'd add, though he doesn't, that it will work equally well for twenty-table restaurants and major mainframe computer makers.

But there is another side to this book. "Systems, Not Smiles" reads one chapter title. Sewell goes on for pages about the importance of apologizing after a foul-up. But he also reveals that his approach—like that of Sam Walton at Wal-Mart and Stew Leonard at Stew Leonard's—is anything but "aw shucks." Sewell turns out, for instance, to be a closet computer-applications pioneer. His servicepeople are quick in large measure because the right part is always available at the right place at exactly the right time—thanks to a peerless and sophisticated inventory management program. Retrieving a customer's car from Sewell's vast lot occurs in no time flat—thanks to yet another computer-aided system.

Sewell measures absolutely everything (see chapter 18). He measures everyone. Furthermore, he puts everyone, including the people who wash your car, on commission. Employee rewards are sky-high and opportunities even higher, but toes are held to a hot fire of high expectation. As at Nordstrom and Apple Computer, Sewell's dealerships are no place to work for the faint of heart.

Carl Sewell provides provocative advice about leadership, from the ins and outs of setting the tone and living your vision to ethics and the celebration of employee successes. He also reveals his secret of success: theft! Sewell jump-started his dealership years ago after a systematic program of identifying and visiting the very best dealers anywhere. Today he gleefully appropriates odds and ends of ideas from Marriott, American Airlines, The Mansion at Turtle Creek, Chuck E. Cheese, Stew Leonard, Neiman Marcus, and a host of others.

I have some worry that Carl, with the help of Paul B. Brown, makes it sound just a little bit too easy. Frankly, his wonderful anecdotes (don't miss the exploding quail) are so colorful that they almost distract from the wise, sophisticated observations about recruiting, pay, motivation, performance measurement systems, and the like. It's hard not to get caught up with the $250 rolls of wallpaper that grace his Cadillac dealership's restrooms, meanwhile ignoring the daily quality meetings, schemes for finding patterns among recurring problems, and Sewell's painstaking study of Japan's quality control masters (he's pioneered in applying their manufacturing ideas to the service sector).

In short, this book is as sophisticated and sober as it is down-home and fun. The language is simple, but the message is anything but simple-minded.

My other problem is that lots of readers will see this as a "car book." Indeed, it's to Sewell's credit that he doesn't use his platform as a successful businessman to pontificate on the national debt, the K-12 education crisis, or even the Cola Wars. He sticks to what he knows. Yet I cannot imagine any business or businessperson (or public agency manager, for that matter) who could not benefit from this book. I plan to give it to friends at Hewlett-Packard and Apple, as well as to retailers, a bevy of bankers, and even a few clergymen.

Hidden beneath the surface of these pages is nothing short of a full-blown theory of management and customer service. It could invigorate any enterprise. I encourage you to dig in, chuckle, ponder—and take action now.

The Ten Commandments
of Customer Service

1 *Bring 'em back alive.*

Ask customers what they want and give it to them again and again.

2 *Systems, not smiles.*

Saying please and thank you doesn't insure you'll do the job right the first time, every time. Only systems guarantee you that.

3 *Underpromise, overdeliver.*

Customers expect you to keep your word. Exceed it.

4 *When the customer asks, the answer is always yes.*

Period.

5 *Fire your inspectors and consumer relations department.*

Every employee who deals with clients must have the authority to handle complaints.

6 *No complaints? Something's wrong.*

Encourage your customers to tell you what you're doing wrong.

7 *Measure everything.*

Baseball teams do it. Football teams do it. Basketball teams do it. You should, too.

8 *Salaries are unfair.*

Pay people like partners.

9 *Your mother was right.*

Show people respect. Be polite. It works.

10 *Japanese them.*

Learn how the best really do it; make their systems your own. Then improve them.

WARNING: *These ten rules aren't worth a damn* . . . unless you make a profit. You have to make money to stay in business and provide good service.

It all starts here:
how good do you want to be?

The Japanese are excellent hosts. While I was in Tokyo recently for the new car show, everyone I met was so gracious, and hospitable that I found it hard to reconcile their politeness with their aggressiveness in business.

I finally figured it out as I stood at the Toyota exhibit and heard a young Japanese engineer explain that their goal was to be "ichiban," (itch-e-bon) which means "number one," the biggest, the best.

I heard that phrase repeatedly, no matter where I went in the country. "This is the biggest bank in the world." "That's the largest brokerage firm." And, of course, we had just left the world's biggest car show.

Now I was born, raised, and still live in Dallas and I thought Texans owned the exclusive rights to being the biggest and best. But we don't anymore. At best, we share it. The Japanese drive to be number one, which seems to govern everything they do, has allowed them to wrestle away at least part of the title from us. "Ichiban" is critical to their success.

And to ours.

The most important thing we ever did at our five car dealerships was decide to be the best. Long before I met my new friends in Japan, the concept of "ichiban" was important to me. Being last stuck in my craw.

I joined Sewell Village Cadillac full time in 1967, after I got out of the Army. Back then there were only three Cadillac dealers in Dallas, and we were third in sales and profits. That bothered the hell out of me. I wanted to be number one.

I didn't know it then, but that decision represented the turning point for our company. Before you can even think about providing better customer service, you must determine how good you want to be. And we were going to be the best.

That decision ended up making life simpler, more fun, and definitely more profitable.

Simpler because it ended a lot of debate. Discussions around here now always boil down to the same question: will doing this make us better? If it will (and if there's any conceivable way to afford it), we'll do it. If it won't, we don't.

Fun because it's more enjoyable to work with people committed to the same objectives. People who don't believe that we have to be the best don't last long around here.

And more profitable because customers now enjoy the way we treat them and want to come back. Instead of buying one car from us, and then disappearing forever, the customer returns whenever he needs a new one.

Over the course of his lifetime he'll end up spending a lot of money with us—$332,000 to be exact.

After a while this way of doing business becomes self-perpetuating.

 * *If you're good to your customers, they'll keep coming back because they like you.*

 * *If they like you, they'll spend more money.*

 * *If they spend more money, you want to treat them better. (You can't do enough for someone who is going to spend $332,000 with you.)*

 * *And if you treat them better, they'll keep coming back and the circle starts again.*

It was Tom Peters who helped quantify the *true* value of a customer for me. Over and over Tom insisted that we stick to our knitting and get closer to our customers.

But it took me awhile to figure how to do it. All I knew at first was that we had to become the best dealership in Dallas. And to do that, I soon understood, we had to figure out a way to differentiate ourselves from the competition.

At first I thought we could be cheaper than everybody else, but that's not really what most people want. Yes, everybody wants a good deal, but price is rarely the sole reason they decide to buy. After you've been to a restaurant, you don't remember exactly what the hamburger cost, you only remember whether you liked it or not.

Besides, we can't compete solely on price. No matter what we charge, somebody—because they're smarter (they figured out a way to be more efficient) or dumber (they don't really know what their costs are)—can always charge a dollar less.

Price wasn't the answer. So I began looking for another solution and, as I did, I started thinking about our company from the customers' point of view. What I realized was most people didn't like doing business with car dealers. They looked forward to seeing us about as much as they did going to the dentist.

I knew that intuitively, but I wasn't sure why. So we started asking customers what they didn't like about doing business with us, and they told us, quite often without mincing words.

They found the service hours—usually 8 A.M. to 5 P.M. Monday through Friday—inconvenient. They thought some of our employees were rude, they hated being without a car while the dealership was working on theirs, and worst of all they often had to bring their car back a second or third time to get a repair done right.

Some of them even pointed out that our grounds were not as clean as they should be, adding our furniture was tired-looking at best, and not very comfortable.

They weren't very specific about how we could improve things, but what they *didn't* like came through loud and clear.

They were telling us what was important. They were defining service excellence.

Once we understood what our customers wanted, we set out to give it to them. We figured if they liked doing business with us—instead of gritting their teeth every time they came in—they'd probably come back more often.

We began by providing them with free loan cars to use while we were working on theirs. We started with 5 loaners and eventually the fleet grew to 257.

Our customers also said they couldn't understand why we wouldn't work on their cars on Saturdays—after all, other stores were open then. In the early 1970s no dealer in the state provided all-day Saturday service. We tried it, and the first weekend twenty-five people thanked me for being open. And to make their lives even easier, we extended our service hours during the week. We now open at 7:30 A.M. and close at 8 P.M.

But some of what they asked for was a lot more difficult to accomplish. How could we make sure the work was always done right? What was the best of way of reducing the time they'd have to spend at the dealership? How could we eliminate every potential problem they might have in doing business with us?

We needed to create systems that would take care of all that, but how? I tried to learn from every source I could find—consultants, books, magazines—but nothing paid off better than visiting successful companies. We spent time with people in the car industry, people like Roger Penske and Bob Moore, but others ran everything from hotels (Marriott and The Mansion on Turtle Creek) to restaurants (McDonald's and Lutèce) to airlines (American and Southwest). We wanted to know how they were able to provide a consistent product and excellent customer service, every time.

We began by visiting with people most like ourselves—other folks who sold cars. We called dozens of people in our industry and asked them who the best automobile dealers were. By actually walking through those dealerships and talking to the people who worked there, we began to understand how the best dealers in the country operated. We asked questions, took pictures, and copied everything we could get our hands on.

We borrowed a lot of ideas. We modified them, and in some cases even improved them, but the basic thoughts came from the people we met and the businesses we visited. Those ideas provided the map for us to follow.

Finally, with our systems in place, we were able to start a program in which we constantly check on how each aspect of our business is doing, and whether we are accomplishing our goals of: being the best, asking customers what they want, and creating systems that allow us to give it to them.

All this is hard as hell. It takes time to visit people and even more time to figure out how to make their ideas work for us. But once we decided our goal was to be the best, we were on the right path.

I'd like to show you how we manage our business and maybe it will help you, whether you're in a big company or just starting out. After all, if our approach to customer service can make the experience of going to a car dealership pleasant, anything's possible.

Customers for Life

ONE

Ask your customers what they want

. . . and give it to 'em

CHAPTER 1

The customer will tell you how to provide good service

We don't assume anything.

We don't, for example, have any rules that say all customers must be greeted in thirty seconds, or that the phone has to be answered by the second ring. Rules like that are created by people who assume they know what customers want. We don't assume anything. Instead, we try to find out. If you give customers a chance to talk, and if you're willing to listen, they'll tell you exactly what's important to them.

In our business—as in most retail businesses—the conventional wisdom is that customers hate to be "attacked" by a salesperson the moment they walk through the door. In fact, we've had consultants tell us we should let customers walk around the showroom for five minutes, "getting acclimated," before anyone goes over to talk to them. I know of some dealerships where that is now a hard and fast rule.

But in all my years as an automobile dealer, I have never had one person complain that our salespeople were too aggressive. I have, however, received far too many letters from people who felt we were not attentive enough.

The point is, it doesn't make any difference what consultants or anybody else say is the right way to greet customers. The only thing that matters is what the customer wants. And the only way to know for sure what they want is to ask them.

Here's how we find out what's on the customer's mind:

First, when she gets to the cashier window, she's asked to answer the three questions on the form that you see on page 4.

The form is short enough so that most people don't mind filling it out. But although it has only three questions, we can learn a lot from it. (Conversely, those same three questions, as you'll see in a minute, are a way for us to get a lot of information across to our customers at the same time.)

WE'D LIKE TO KNOW . . . .

1. ARE THE CHARGES (LESS THAN), (THE SAME AS), (MORE THAN) the FINAL ESTIMATE? (Please circle one.)

2. WAS YOUR AUTOMOBILE READY WHEN PROM- ISED?

    _____ Yes   _____ No

3. IS THIS THE SECOND TIME FOR THE SAME REPAIR?

    _____ No   _____ Yes

THANK YOU VERY MUCH ! !

_____

_____

_____

SEWELL
Village Cadillac
STERLING
A family tradition since 1911.

Question 1 is there because if people don't think they're getting good value for their money, they won't enjoy doing business with us, no matter what we do.

Question 2 is designed to find out if we kept our word. *Was* the car ready when we promised?

And finally, question 3 allows us to discover if we had to do the same repair over again.

Those three questions get to the heart of every service transaction, and with a little modification they could be asked by almost every business.

In evaluating an ad agency, for example, the questions might be: 1) Was the campaign within budget? 2) Did it come in on time? 3) Did it work?

The secret—whether you are selling advertising or automobiles—is to identify the three things that are most important to the customer.

Once we know what's important, we then have to make sure we're providing it. So we measure it.

If customers think they paid more than they should have, or if the car wasn't ready when we said it would be, or this was the second (or third) time they had to come back for the same repair, then we aren't doing a very good job. We should know that. If they tell us we haven't done a good job, we have a chance to apologize on the spot. If the bill was higher, or the car wasn't ready, the cashier summons a manager, who comes out right then, apologizes, and immediately arranges to have the work redone.

However, most of the time we do a pretty good job, and the form lets us remind our customers of that—without bragging. Answering the questions underscores that the bill *was less* than the estimate. It also reminds people the car *was* ready when promised and we did the work right the first time.

The overall purpose of these three questions is to point out that our dealerships really do care about their customers.

You'll notice that at the end of the form we say that we've been around since 1911. To be honest, I don't think too many people give us points for that. The attitude of most folks is: "What have you done for me lately?"

But we're proud of our history, and of the company my father started, and maybe, when people see that we've been in business for more than three quarters of a century, they'll think: "That means they'll probably be here if I have a problem."

The other thing you'll notice about the form is that we leave a place on the bottom where people can write in comments.

If they have the time, and the desire, another way they can give us their opinions is by filling in the 49-question customer service survey that we include in the folder that contains their bill. A copy of the form is on pages 8–9.

(A confession. For many years we carefully surveyed our new car customers, without ever trying to find out what used car customers liked —or didn't like—about doing business with us. That was dumb. Used car customers are every bit as important as new car customers to our success because they, too, have the potential to become $332,000 customers. I don't think we were alone in forgetting about a certain segment of our customers—nonetheless, we don't forget about them anymore.

By all means ask customers what they want, but ask politely, and don't force them to answer. Present surveys in such a way that customers can ignore them if they don't want to participate.

The surveys are strictly optional. We could have gotten the same information by calling our customers at home, but I don't like to get those kinds of calls. It seems they always come right when I am in the middle of dinner or playing softball with the kids. I think most of our customers feel the same way I do. So we don't do phone surveys. Instead we give customers something they can fill out and send to us, if they want. (About 35% of them complete the 49-question survey and send it back.) If they don't want to, they can throw it in the trash.

We don't want to bother our customers. We give them every opportunity to tell us what they think, but we make it optional. If they don't want to tell us, that's fine. If they do want to tell us, we try to make it as easy for them as possible. We offer them the chance to answer three questions at the cashier window. We have the longer questionnaire they can fill out if they want, and if they still have more to tell us, we—as the last thing on the 49-question survey points out—ask them if they'd like to be part of a focus group.

Focus groups are an idea we borrowed directly from Stew Leonard and Stew Leonard, Jr., who told us how to do them.

Focus groups are extremely effective. They're a check to see how well you're doing, because you're asking customers how they like doing business with you. Are you really giving them all the things you think you are, or are you falling down in ways you don't know about?

There's another reason we use them. Focus groups help us keep tabs on things.

As we grew, I realized management by wandering around (MBWA) is effective when you have one store, even two. You can see what's going on.

But it doesn't work as well when you have multiple locations, because you can't spend enough time wandering around each one. You need additional sources of information, like focus groups.

We had perceived focus groups to be some kind of voodoo magic, and it turns out they're not. They're really pretty simple. We (either I or one of our senior managers) get ten or twelve people in a room and start asking questions about how they like doing business with us, what they see as our strengths and weaknesses. After that, we get zeroed in on a special area. One time we'll ask 10 questions or so about service work. (Those questions are lifted right from the 49-question customer service survey.) Another time we'll talk about the sales experience. Did you feel comfortable talking with us? Did we know our product? Did your sales person call you back within two weeks to make sure your purchase was okay?

In total, we probably spend an hour and a half with a focus group, say thank you, and give them a Cross pen set as they leave. The customers like to be involved.

When we pick people to invite, we make sure they're representative of our customers, or people we would like to be our customers. That means we do four or five focus groups on a particular subject to ensure we get an accurate response.

When we first started doing focus groups, I was skeptical. I didn't think people would say anything negative about us, especially when we were sitting in the room with them. But I was wrong. There really is safety in numbers. There are a lot of people in that room, and the longer the meeting goes on, the more likely you are to hear some honest comments. In the second or third half hour, all of a sudden somebody will say, "Let me tell you how it really is," and from then on you know you're going to hear the truth.

Oh, occasionally you hear some bull. But we try to apply a little statistical logic to help sort that out. If we talk to 100 people, invariably we'll get somebody all the way out in right field and somebody all the way out in left. That's okay. But we always ask, "what do we have in the middle that's really strong?" That's what we pay attention to.

Another thing I've learned is: don't ignore a deeply held reaction, just because it's not the majority view. When Ford was researching the Taurus, they found that about half the people loved the way it looked and half hated it, so you had a final approval rating of somewhere around 4.5 out of 10. But remember, half the people really loved it. And half—when you're talking about the number of people who buy cars—is a hell of a big number. So Ford went ahead with production.

You can take that a step further. Sometimes it's worth paying attention to a comment, even if only one person makes it. I remember we did a focus group at Hyundai, and a man said he hated our loan car program, because when he showed up for service he was told we didn't have any loan cars. He was the only person who said that had happened to him,

Q U E S T I O N N A I R E

1. Approximately how many times have you used our Service Department within the past year?
_____ times

WHEN YOU LAST USED OUR SERVICE DEPARTMENT:

2. Did you have difficulty in finding the Service Department?
Yes _____ No _____

3. When you arrived at the service area, were you greeted promptly?
Yes _____ No _____

4. How were you treated when you entered our service reception area?
Very professionally __ Somewhat professionally __
Not at all professionally __

5. After you were greeted, approximately how long did you have to wait until your Service Adviser was available?
_____ minutes

6. Did you feel that the period of time you waited for your Service Adviser was excessive?
Yes _____ No _____

7. Did your Service Adviser explain things to you clearly?
Yes _____ No _____

8. Were you given a cost estimate of the charges for your automobile?
Yes _____ No _____

9. Were you given a time estimate as to when your automobile would be ready?
Yes _____ No _____

10. Sewell Village have various methods of payment available. Was this discussed with you?
Yes _____ No _____

11. Overall, how would you rate your satisfaction with your Service Adviser?
Very satisfied __ Somewhat satisfied __
Neither satisfied nor dissatisfied __
Somewhat dissatisfied __ Very dissatisfied __

12. Are you aware that if you purchased your automobile *new* from Sewell Village, you can reserve a loan car?
Yes _____ No _____
(If NO, skip to Q.15)

13. Are you familiar with the procedure of reserving a loan car?
Yes _____ No _____
(If NO, skip to Q.15)

14. Did you call to reserve a loan car?
Yes _____ No _____
(If NO, skip to Q.15)

14a. Did you feel that the loan car personnel were friendly?
Yes _____ No _____

14b. Was a loan car available when you needed it?
Yes _____ No _____

14c. Was there adequate gasoline in the loan car when you received it?
Yes _____ No _____

15. When you last used our Service Department, did you use our Courtesy Car?
Yes _____ No _____
(If NO, skip to Q.19)

16. How satisfied were you with the cleanliness of the Courtesy Car?
Very satisfied __ Somewhat satisfied __
Neither satisfied nor dissatisfied __
Somewhat dissatisfied __ Very dissatisfied __

17. Approximately how long did you wait for the Courtesy Car?
_____ minutes

18. Was the driver of the Courtesy Car professional?
Yes _____ No _____

19. When you last visited our Service Department, did you use our waiting area?
Yes _____ No _____
(If NO, skip to Q.22)

20. Was our waiting area clean?
Yes _____ No _____

21. Was adequate seating available?
Yes _____ No _____

22. Did we call to inform you that your automobile was ready?
Yes _____ No _____
(If YES, skip to Q.25)

23. How many rings did it take us to answer the telephone?
#_____ rings

24. Did we return your calls promptly?
Yes _____ No _____

25. Were we polite over the telephone?
Yes _____ No _____

26. Were we helpful over the telephone?
Yes _____ No _____

27. Was the repair/service completed correctly the first time your automobile was brought in?
Yes _____ No _____

28. How would you describe your satisfaction with the repair/service at Sewell Village?
Very satisfied __ Somewhat satisfied __
Neither satisfied nor dissatisfied __
Somewhat dissatisfied __ Very dissatisfied __

29. Was your automobile ready when promised?
Yes _____ No _____

30. Approximately how long did you have to wait in line at the Cashier window?
_____ minutes

31. Was the cashier polite?
Yes _____ No _____

32. Was the cashier helpful?
Yes _____ No _____

33. If you had questions about what was done to your automobile, were we able to answer those questions?
Yes _____ No _____

34. Were the actual repair/service charges less than or the same as the *final* estimate?
Yes _____ No _____

35. To your knowledge, were all applicable warranties considered and applied to the repairs?
　　　Yes _____ No _____

36. After you left the Cashier window, approximately how long did you wait for your automobile?
　　　_____ minutes

37. Did the cashier clearly explain where your automobile would be delivered?
　　　Yes _____ No _____

38. Was there a person waiting for you at your automobile when it was brought up to you?

　　　Yes _____ No _____
　　　　　(If NO, skip to Q.42)

39. Was that person friendly?
　　　Yes _____ No _____

40. How would you rate that person's appearance?
　　　Excellent _____ Good _____
　　　Average _____ Poor _____

41. Did that person say "thank you"?
　　　Yes _____ No _____

42. Did we get your automobile dirty during its servicing?
　　　Yes _____ No _____

43. Overall, how satisfied are you with Sewell Village's Service Department?
　　　Very satisfied ___ Somewhat satisfied ___
　　　　Neither satisfied nor dissatisfied ___
　　　Somewhat dissatisfied ___ Very dissatisfied ___

44. Did you buy your automobile from Sewell Village?
　　　Yes _____ No _____

44a. If "yes," did you purchase your car new or used?
　　　New _____ Used _____

44b. If purchased elsewhere, which dealer?
_____

45. What is the model of your automobile?
　　　19_____

46. Would you recommend the Sewell Village Service Department to a friend?
　　　Yes _____ No _____

47. What is your Service Adviser's name?
_____

48. Did any one staff member, through outstanding service, make your visit more enjoyable? _____
_____
_____

49. Would you be interested in participating in our advisory panel?
　　　Yes _____ No _____

Do you have any suggestions as to how Sewell Village could better serve you?

_____
_____
_____
_____
_____
_____
_____
_____

Thank you for taking the time to tell us about your service experience at Sewell Village. Our Quality Statement is: We will deliver 100% defect-free goods and services on time.

SEWELL
Village Cadillac
STERLING
A family tradition since 1911.

7310 Lemmon Ave. at University. 350-2000

and our general manager swore he always had cars available, but there was something about the way the customer said it that rang true. I couldn't figure out why he would make up something like that.

So I did a little checking and found out that a number of times the general manager *was* turning people away. Instead of ordering more loan cars, he would tell people to come back when one of the loaners he had was available.

We replaced that general manager and now, if we tell you there will be loan cars available at Hyundai, there will be.

People *will* tell you the truth. If they've filled out a 49-question survey, and taken the time to show up at a focus group, they really want to tell you how they feel. We listen very carefully.

CHECKLIST

✔ *Don't guess about what customers want.* They're more than willing to tell you.

✔ *Make it easy for them to tell you.* Create a short questionnaire—no more than 5 questions, preferably 3—that focuses on the most important parts of doing business with you from the customer's point of view.

✔ *An easy way to get 100% response . . .* is to give customers that short survey when they pay. That way, they can fill it out while you're totaling their bill.

✔ *Don't pester them.* If people don't want to fill out surveys or answer questions, that's fine. Don't force them to. Don't start calling them up at night or hassling them when they are in the store. Remember, the whole idea behind asking them questions is to create a place where people are going to be happy to do business. If you pester them, they're not going to be happy.

CHAPTER 2

If the customer asks,
the answer is always yes

For our way of doing business to work, we have to convince you that there is something more valuable than money. After all, we're not the cheapest, so to be successful we must offer you something else. That something is convenience. We remove hassles. We try to make your life easier.

Any time a customer asks if it's possible for us to do something, the answer is yes. If you lock yourself out of the car or you get a flat, and you call up and ask if we can help, we're going to respond, "Sure thing."

We're probably not going to paint your house or wash your windows. We sell automobiles. However, if the request relates to our business, we're going to try to do it. Whenever possible we want to help our customers.

Here's my favorite example. We have an excellent customer who lives half the year in Dallas and the other half in France. When she was coming back from Paris last year she called us up and said she planned to spend some time in New York before returning home, but she didn't want to rent a car there. She said all New York rental cars were dirty and smelled of cigarette smoke. She wanted to know if we could rent a car for her in Dallas and have someone drive it to New York, and turn it over to her there. We could, and we did.

If the customer asks if you can do something for him, the answer is always yes, providing the request is somehow related to your business.

When we talk to some people about this way of doing business, they look at us funny. They say when we're extending ourselves—running around trying to find a driver for a customer who has bought a limousine from us—we're not doing our "regular" job. But of course we are. Our job is to take care of the customer so well that he keeps coming back to us for the rest of his life.

Say you arrived at the airport at nine o'clock at night and the key broke off in the lock when you tried to open the door. You call your wife and she's not home. You'd be stuck.

Now imagine what would happen if you then called our dealership and we immediately sent a truck out, and the technician made a key for you right there, said, "Thank you for remembering us," and then drove away without taking any money. You'd think we were pretty good guys.

Do we ever charge for doing all this?

Sometimes, but generally not. Our rule of thumb: is this something a friend would charge for? If you locked yourself out of your car and you called a friend, would he charge you for running a key over? No. Well, we won't either.

That's just common sense. But let's talk about why this makes economic sense, too.

Let's say it costs us $25 to go over and let that customer into his car. Think about the cost of a radio ad. In Dallas, during peak drive times, a sixty-second commercial on a popular station costs $700.

For the $25 we spent letting you into your car, I probably have a customer for life. How many customers for life am I going to get from a $700 radio ad? I'd need 28—$700 divided by 28 equals $25—to get the same results from the ad that I got from helping that customer at the airport. Common sense tells me we're not going to get 28 customers for life from one radio commercial.

Now, is everything free? Of course not. If we have to go out and install a battery and an alternator, we're going to charge you normal rates, plus the call. But if it's something unusual, like breaking off a key, we won't charge. We'll just help. If we're able to help our customers, they'll want to do business with us again and again and again.

CHECKLIST

✔ *The moment the customer says, "Can you . . ."* you should be pre-pared to answer yes, even if you can't immediately figure out how to do what she wants.

✔ *Stretch.* You cut lawns for a living, and your customer needs the name of a good tree surgeon? Find him one. If he is staying at your hotel, and his car gets a flat, change it. Help your customer.

✔ *Don't charge for this "extra" service if you can help it.* If it's something that a friend would do for another friend, don't charge. Don't worry, you'll more than make up the money in future business.

CHAPTER

There's no such thing
as after hours

Customer service is a 24-hour-a-day deal. It has to be. First off, customers will, upon occasion, ask you to do something after 5 P.M. or on a Sunday. And if the rule is: "When the customer says, 'Can you?' the answer is always yes," it has to be yes then too.

But there's a second and more basic reason why there's no such thing as after hours. How can we be giving customers the best service if we're forcing them to conform to our schedule? By definition, that has to be inconvenient for them sometimes.

We have to work when they want us to, not when we want to.

So that's what we do. We're happy to deliver cars (complete with bows on them, if you like) to people's homes on birthdays, anniversaries, and Christmas Eve—even if those days fall on a Sunday or holiday.

We'll be happy to meet someone here at the dealership on Sunday morning and give them a private showing, and if they want to show up in their pajamas, that's fine with us.

You need to come at nine o'clock at night, and we close at eight? No problem. We'll wait.

Some people might view all this as a pain in the backside, but we don't. By adjusting to fit our customers' schedules, we get to sell them a car—and maybe, long term, more than one.

Now can this get to be inconvenient? Sure. But does the customer care that we might be late for dinner? No, and what the customer wants is the only thing that matters.

We want to make his life as easy as possible. Let's take what happens at our Cadillac dealership, for example.

As a rule, all of our salespeople and service advisers give out their home telephone numbers. They want to be able to help you when you need help. If you lose the number or don't have it with you when you need it, it's no big deal. All you have to do is call the dealership. We have a police officer who's there after we've locked up for the night, and he has everybody's number. You call, and he'll arrange to have the right person take care of you.

Let's say it's five in the morning, you're leaving for work, and you discover you have a flat. (We get a lot of calls like that.) You call the showroom, and the policeman will phone the service technician on call —somebody is available 24 hours a day, every day—and he'll drive over in the Chevy Suburban that we've turned into a repair truck, and take care of you. (The Suburban has an air compressor, key cutter, and everything else you can possibly imagine, right on board.) The technician will put your spare on—and, as we've said, won't charge you for it—and you'll be on your way.

We want people to call us, no matter what time it is. They're our customers, and we want to take care of them. Besides, we would rather do the work than have our customers give it to somebody who might charge more and care less.

No matter what business you're in, customers like to have a number to call after hours.

The biggest problem we have with this is that customers forget, or don't believe, we'll take care of them no matter what. We tell them all the time. We give them stickers with our 24-hour-a-day phone number on it, and still they don't call us. We want them to call. They're our customers and we want to take care of them.

Still, they scramble for their service station, a wrecker, or whatever they need. They just forget to call.

Can the people who do call take advantage of us? Sure, but that doesn't happen often.

Almost every time someone calls us "after hours," it's because they need help and they need it immediately. If they need help, we should provide it, no matter what time it is. It gives us a chance to maintain our relationship with the customer, by doing something for him, and people really like the service.

CHECKLIST

✔ *You can't just provide service between 9 A.M. and 5 P.M.* If you're going to provide good service, you have to provide it around the clock.

✔ *One call should do it all.* Make it easy for customers to get that service. They shouldn't have to call all over at 3 A.M. looking for someone to help them. A single phone call to you is all it should take. You don't have to give out your home phone number (although customers like it if you do). And you don't have to have someone sitting at the switchboard 24 hours a day. Do what doctors do: hire an answering service. Have the service field the calls that come in after normal business hours. After taking the message, the service can then call whoever is on duty.

✔ *Don't worry about people taking advantage of you.* As a rule, they'll only call if they really need help.

CHAPTER 4

Underpromise, overdeliver

Every time you bring your car in, we give you a *guaranteed* estimate of what we will charge you to fix your car. And there is a tendency on the part of the service adviser to make the estimate as low as possible. He's afraid we'll lose the business if the customer thinks the price quote is too high.

But we don't want our service advisers to worry about that. In fact, we ask them to build a 10% cushion into every estimate. That way, we can ensure that the final bill will always be less than what we quoted. At the very worst, we are always, always, always at least $1 less than the estimate. The result? Happy customers.

One of the worst things you can do is charge a customer more than your estimate. Build in a cushion so you can always charge a little less.

Here's how it works. If you bring in your car for a repair that we think will cost $90, our estimate will be $100. When you come to pick up your car and find out you only have to pay $90, you're really happy.

The idea here is not to rip people off. If it's a $90 job, we'll charge $85, even though we quoted $100 and the customer didn't complain. Could we get that additional $10? Sure, once or twice. But as my cousin John Sewell, who ran our Cadillac dealership, always said: "You can shear a sheep for many years, but you can only skin it once."

The customer will eventually figure out he's being skinned, and you'll never see him again.

Now the problem is that sometimes the customer service advisers get nervous that you might not take the $100 estimate, and they'll quote $90. If the final bill ends up being $91, you won't like it.

But if we quoted $100, thinking it was going to be a $90 job, and it ended up costing $91, you wouldn't mind. The job still cost $9 less than we told you it would. The nice thing about this approach is that it gives us a safety factor, in case the job costs a little more than we thought.

It also allows us to do a little bit extra for the customer, without charging him. Say that while we're doing that $90 job, we find that the windshield wipers needed replacing. That normally runs about $7. Well, we can replace them and *still* give the customer back his car with a bill that will be less than what we quoted him. Now the customer is happy for two reasons: we did some additional work, *and* we still charged less than the estimate. (In this case, the bill would have been $97, the $90 the job actually cost, plus $7 for the wipers.)

The risk with this approach, of course, is that there are some folks who will think the initial $100 estimate is too high, and take their business elsewhere. But that may be 1% or 2% of the people. And if they really feel that way, then we're not the folks they should be doing business with.

There are people who tell us that our price on a lube, oil and filter is $9 more than they would pay if they took their car to Quickie Lube and waited for it there. And that's true. We are not the cheapest, but we are the best. You know if you bring the car to us, not only will the bill be less than we quoted, but we'll do the job right.

Our pricing policy seems to be one that most people are comfortable with. They know we're never going to charge them more than we quoted. People like doing business with people who keep their word.

CHECKLIST

✔ *Build in a cushion.* Always estimate high—10% more than you think the job will actually cost. That way, your final bill can easily be lower than the price quote. By doing that, you've also built in a safety factor in case the estimate is off. But in either case, *always* present a bill that at the very least is $1 less than the estimate.

✔ *No windfall profits.* If the actual cost is less than the estimate, charge the lower amount. Period. Keeping the difference is not as good as keeping the customer.

✔ *Throw in some extras if you can.* Since you have built in a cushion, you can afford to do some additional work (if it's needed) without being forced to charge more than you promised.

TWO

How to give good service every time

CHAPTER 5

Systems, not smiles

When people think of customer service, it's usually the warm fuzzy things that come to mind: saying please and thank you; yes, ma'am, and no, sir; calling another store to see if they have the item in stock.

That's certainly part of providing good service—but it's only a small part. If customer service were a cake, the politeness, smiles, and being willing to go the extra mile would be the icing. The cake would be the systems that allow you to do a good job.

Doing a good job has two parts:

1) doing the job right the first time; and

2) having a plan in place to deal with things when they go wrong.

Having systems that allow you to do both those things are more important than all the warm and fuzzy feelings in the world. After all, it doesn't make any difference to our customers how nice we are if we don't do the job right or, at the very least, immediately take care of the problem when something goes wrong.

It's like going to a restaurant. They can smile till their jaws ache, hold your chair for you when you sit down, and refold your napkin every time you leave the table, but if the food is no good, you're not likely to go back.

What's needed in restaurants, car dealerships, department stores, and every place else is systems—not just smiles—that guarantee good service.

Every business is composed of a group of systems. Those systems must work together to create a process that is efficient and responsive to a customer's wants.

Systems have always been an integral part of manufacturing. Without carefully planned and measured processes, there's no way to make anything efficiently.

In the automobile industry, for example, the people with process-oriented minds usually are engineers. And as a rule, they tend to go into either design or manufacturing. There are thousands of engineers who have spent their entire lives studying manufacturing processes—just-in-time inventory systems, statistical process controls, and manufacturing processing theory. They apply these systems when they're building cars.

Service companies should employ this same kind of systematic thinking, but most service consultants spend too much time on "smiles" instead of systems.

The folks who wind up in service or sales rarely are engineers. They've never studied subjects like material handling and statistical process controls, and there's little likelihood they'll be able to discuss the latest theory of inventory management.

Being nice to people is just 20% of providing good customer service. The important part is designing systems that allow you to do the job right the first time. All the smiles in the world aren't going to help you if your product or service is not what the customer wants.

But they should know about them, because applying those kinds of systems—which are designed to eliminate every possible variation—is the most efficient way of improving the service you provide. The writings of people like Edwards Deming, Eliyahu M. Goldratt (*The Goal*), Taiichi Ohno, the man who set up Toyota's manufacturing systems, and Genichi Taguchi are wonderful resources to draw on to create efficient service systems.

Still, the best story I ever heard about systems concerned McDonald's and their french fries.

When McDonald's began their quest to serve the perfect french fry every time, there were no national standards for potatoes. The U. S. Department of Agriculture didn't have a grading system which said, This is a good potato, that one's better, and the one over there is awful.

In addition, no one knew exactly how hot the grease used to fry the potato should be, or how you could guarantee that temperature would remain constant during cooking or how the potatoes should be stored to keep them from spoiling.

By the time McDonald's finished, they had helped establish the quality standards for the Department of Agriculture. They knew what kind of soil the potatoes should be grown in to achieve the consistency they wanted. They even created their own frying equipment to ensure that the potatoes cooked the same way every time.

To me this story exemplifies customer service. By devoting all that time and attention to the ways potatoes are grown, stored, and cooked, McDonald's has virtually guaranteed that the fries they serve you will be good every time.

They're consistently good because almost every variable that could cause them to be less than perfect has been eliminated. As Taguchi says: The more variations you can eliminate, the better your product or service will be. After all, when you go to Lutèce you want your favorite dessert to taste the same every time. In McDonald's case, eliminating all the variations meant going all the way back to the soil the potatoes were grown in and figuring out how acidic it should be.

All over the country the best service people have started thinking like McDonald's. Take inventory management. The idea behind it is really pretty basic: if you don't have in stock what the customer wants, you can't give it to him. And if you can't give the customer what he wants, you haven't provided good service.

Wal-Mart provides *great* service: it also has the best inventory system of any retailer anywhere.

Every item in the store is bar-coded, and as it's sold, that fact is recorded at the checkout counter. At the end of the day, the data from all Wal-Mart registers is sent not only to Wal-Mart warehouses but also to the company's suppliers. That way, if the store is running low on something, the manufacturer can ship it out the next day.

Contrast that with what happens at other stores, where the buyer periodically submits orders to the manufacturer. In between orders the manufacturer has little idea what's selling.

Under Wal-Mart's system, that doesn't happen. The warehouse and the manufacturers know how many items were sold every day and what needs to be reordered, and what doesn't. This reduces inventory costs tremendously.

Wal-Mart took this a step further, though. They have their manufacturers pack their containers so that, when they get to the store, it's easy for the stocker to put the merchandise out in a logical and functional manner. (All the sweaters are packed next to shirts, for example.) Plus, the stocker checks in the inventory using a bar code reader. He doesn't have to count anything, and there's nothing to write down. Since the items are checked in automatically, there's no chance of anything being coded incorrectly.

I wish we could say the same things about cars. Most automobiles have 17-character Vehicle Identification numbers. And there's a good chance that if you write down 100 VI numbers in a day, you are going to make a mistake on at least one of them. After all, you are talking about 1,700 chances of making an error (the 17 letters times the 100 cars) and even if you got everything right 99.9% of the time, that's almost 2 mistakes per 100 VI numbers. Where's the consistency in that? Obviously, Wal-Mart's bar coding approach is much better.

Do you know who explained Wal-Mart's inventory system to me? David Glass, Wal-Mart's president. That's the importance Wal-Mart assigns to inventory systems—which really are another form of customer service. The company president is involved in creating them and making sure they work.

Systematic approaches are 80% of customer service. They're what's *really* important, not the smiles and thank yous. The key is to devise systems that allow you to give the customer what he wants every time.

CHECKLIST

✔ *What can go wrong?* That's the question to ask in designing your systems. Examine every step you take in delivering your product or service, and see where there are possibilities for error or variation. Then figure out ways to eliminate them.

✔ *What can be automated?* By using computers wherever possible, you not only increase the speed of each transaction, you also decrease the chance for human error.

✔ *Look to manufacturers, if you want to provide good service.* Manufacturers, not service companies, have the best systems. They should be your models.

CHAPTER 6

Fire your inspectors

Inspectors make people sloppy. If you know someone is checking your work, you might not check it yourself. We learned that lesson the hard way.

After going for years without having quality inspectors, and getting scores on the General Motors Customer Satisfaction Index (CSI) in the high 90s, we decided that the best way to ensure 100% quality was to do 100% inspection. That way, we would be able to catch the few problems that were getting by.

So we started adding inspectors. Eventually we got up to seven, and we inspected every job at every turn. And you know what happened? Our CSI, and our quality, went down.

Because we had all those inspectors, our technicians stopped feeling as responsible for their work. They felt it wasn't up to them anymore to make sure the job they did was absolutely right. That's what the inspectors were for, they said.

The technicians had lost pride in what they were doing.

The moment we took away all those inspectors, our CSI went up and so did the quality of the work. It's now the best it's ever been because our people feel more responsible for their work, and they like that feeling.

If a job is done wrong, the person who made the mistake must fix it and he shouldn't be paid for setting it right. Since the company doesn't get paid for doing a job over, neither should the person who did it wrong.

And on those rare occasions where one of us does a job that is less than perfect we all suffer together.

If a customer brings the car back, whoever did the job wrong initially is going to do it over without being paid for that second repair. That's only fair because "comebacks" hurt not only the customer—who is inconvenienced—but the company.

The dealership suffers, because our reputation is tarnished. Plus, we aren't getting paid for setting things right. In fact, making the repair actually costs us money, because we still have to pay for heat, power, water, rent, and taxes while we are making the repair for free.

Since we don't make any money for doing the work over, neither does the person who did it wrong.

Each comeback is also going to be talked about in our morning quality meeting, and the technician's manager is going to be discussing it with him as well.

So the technician will know the job came back, we will know it came back, and we will know why it came back.

Now, sometimes, it's not the technician's fault. You can install a light bulb, and it can work fine for twenty-four hours and then quit of its own mind. I worked as an inspector, and I passed many cars that were perfect when they left here but came back because whatever we did didn't hold.

But the customer doesn't care what caused the problem or how many people approved the repair. If the work isn't done right, she's going to bring it back.

Now, no matter what we do, and no matter how diligent everyone is, there will be problems. It's inevitable. We're all human and make mistakes. And despite all their quality assurance programs, manufacturers still—upon occasion—let a defective product slip through.

But instead of simply shrugging our shoulders and saying, "Mistakes will happen," we keep track of what work has to be redone, and after we fix the job for the customer, we try to fix the flaw in our systems that allowed the problem to slip through.

That's important. We found out a long time ago that if we just respond to problems our quality suffers.

Sure we have to fix problems, but if that's all we do, we're going to keep having the same problems over and over again. It's more efficient to find out what caused the problem in the first place—we do what's sometimes described as a root cause analysis—and correct the process once and for all. What we've found is that the process must be right and the worker must have the necessary knowledge and support to do his job correctly.

Here's an example. We had a technician who did absolutely wonderful work, with one exception. Every time he tried to repair fuel injectors, he'd never get it quite right.

When you have this kind of problem, what you can do, of course, is keep re-repairing those fuel injectors, every time a customer complains. Or you can try to find out what the root cause of the problem is. Often the solution is simple, as it was in this case. The technician had never learned the proper way to do the repair. So we showed him. As Deming says, you can only know what you know.

Once we identify the problem, we classify it by type of job, technician and service adviser. Then we look for patterns. Are we getting a lot of complaints about all of our fuel injector repairs? If we are, when was the last time our technicians received training on how to fix them?

Maybe all the complaints can be traced back to one service adviser. Maybe he isn't diagnosing the problem correctly when the customer brings it in.

We make it easy to track errors in the sales department, too. For example, we ask our people to present each new or used car to its new owner with a full tank of gas. And when they deliver the car, we ask them to schedule the customer's first service appointment. If we find out those things weren't done, we know who disappointed the customer and we know whom to talk to—the salesperson who sold them the car.

If you fix the system, the problem is eliminated for good.

CHECKLIST

✔ *If you have inspectors, get rid of them.* Inspectors don't improve quality.

✔ *Don't pay people twice for the same job.* No one—neither the company nor the worker—should make money if a job has to be redone. Service excellence and quality assurance should be a partnership.

✔ *Talk about the mistakes.* Log every single job that is brought back. As soon as it comes in, fix it. Then find out how the problem was able to slip through in the first place.

✔ *Hold daily quality meetings* . . . to ensure you have a chance to talk about problems. These meetings should not be for managers only. Invite the people who actually do the work and deal with customers. They're the ones who usually know what is going on.

✔ *Look for patterns.* Collect enough information so that over time you can spot trends and problem areas.

CHAPTER 7

Fire your consumer relations department, too

As long as you're getting rid of your inspectors, you might as well fire your consumer relations representatives, too. Customer service is just too important to be left to a "consumer relations" department.

Everybody should be a customer service rep and, in fact, that's how the customer sees it anyway. Customers judge the service they receive by how well they're treated by *everybody* they come in contact with. If the cashier is rude, or the salesperson isn't helpful, the customer thinks he has gotten terrible service, no matter how friendly, warm, and helpful the people in the customer service department might be. And he's right. He *has* gotten terrible service.

The people who deal with customers must have the authority to resolve problems.

And that brings up an interesting point. There's an old Texas saying that the footprint of the farmer is the best fertilizer—meaning that the way to ensure that everything goes smoothly is to make sure the farmer (or, in my case, the owner) is always there to deal with every customer. And that is certainly one way to ensure great customer service. Who better than the owner to make sure that customers are taken care of?

But the problem with that is obvious. If the owner is going to deal with every customer, the business can't get any bigger than what one person can handle. To extend the analogy, the farmer wouldn't be able to manage more than one farm.

It seems more effective for the farmer (boss) to make *everyone* a customer service representative. Tell everyone in the company: If a customer has a problem, solve it. If you can't solve it, get your manager. If he can't solve it, give it to the CEO, but get the problem solved. Immediately.

This can be a difficult concept to get across, especially if you're part of a large organization. About fifteen years ago, GM came out with a customer service program. As part of it, they said they wanted a "consumer relations" manager at every GM dealership. However, we chose not to have one.

The *idea* behind having consumer relations departments is not bad. It shows you care, and that you want to take care of the people who do business with you. It's just that you can take care of your customers more efficiently, and in a way that will make your employees happier, if you don't have a separate customer service department. We debated that point with GM for years.

Then the Customer Satisfaction Index scores came out, and our CSI was better than those of the dealerships with consumer relations managers, so GM decided that we weren't quite so bad after all.

The number one priority at our dealerships is customer satisfaction. No matter what your job, if you don't make the customer happy, you won't work here for long. That is made very clear. You can be the best salesperson, or the most productive technician, but if your CSI is not good, you are history, because if the customer doesn't want to come back none of us will have a job.

CHECKLIST

✔ *Consumer relations departments separate you from the customer.* So don't have one.

✔ *Let your employees take care of their customers.* If every employee is a customer service representative, then every employee should have the power to satisfy the customer.

✔ *Nothing is more important than the customer.* Employees must know that no matter how many sales they make, or how productive they are, if they mistreat their customers (or their fellow employees) they will be fired.

Do it right the first time

Leonard L. Berry is the director of the Center for Retailing Studies at Texas A&M. He's also a friend. Len has spent just about all his professional life talking to people, trying to find out what they want in terms of customer service. And after all this time he's concluded that there's nothing more important to the customer than "keeping the service promise."

"Customer expectations of service providers are loud and clear," Berry tells his students and the corporations who hire him as a consultant. "Customers want service organizations to look good, be responsive, be reassuring, be empathetic, and most of all—be reliable. *Customers want firms to do what they say they are going to do.*"

The emphasis in that quote is his, and it's well deserved. Nothing makes a customer madder than a business that doesn't do what it promises.

Think about People Express. The idea behind the company was great. They would fly you between point A and point B for almost nothing—$19 in some cases. They squeezed you into their no-frills plane and made you pay $3 for each bag you had checked, and fifty cents if you wanted a cup of coffee during the flight, but their customers didn't mind, because they were going to fly where they wanted to go for less than it would have cost to take the bus.

It was a great idea. But People Express eventually failed, and the reason is simple. The company didn't keep its word. The planes were constantly late, and you never knew for sure, when you showed up at the airport, whether they were actually going to take off at all. People Express didn't keep what Len Berry calls the service promise.

The best system in the world for providing customer service is also the simplest: DO WHAT YOU SAY YOU ARE GOING TO DO, AND DO IT RIGHT THE FIRST TIME.

Too often when people talk about customer service, they spend their time explaining what to do after someone screws up.

How you make amends for doing something wrong is important, of course, but if you do the job right initially, you don't have anything to apologize for. At the very least, good customer service requires you to do the job right the first time.

Lexus is the best example of that. Conventional wisdom among new car buyers has always been: "Don't buy a new car in its introductory year. Give 'em a year to get the bugs out."

But today consumers no longer give manufacturers a grace period. They have no reason to wait. There are too many quality products already out there. You either get it right the first time or risk being left behind forever.

Lexus, under the leadership of Dave Illingworth and Ted Toyoda, got it right. They spent seven years in "the relentless pursuit of perfection." They built 400 prototypes, instead of the usual 12, and they focus–grouped the car extensively. Dave consistently worked 100-hour weeks and Ted moved his family to the United States at the beginning of the project to make sure nothing was overlooked. Nothing was. They got it right the first time.

The most important thing to a customer is: Did you do what you promised? Keeping your word is worth more than all the empathy, smiles, and chocolates on your pillow in the world.

Doing what you're supposed to do, when you're supposed to do it, is such a simple way of providing customer service that people tend to forget about it. But everybody likes things to go smoothly. The problem is that they don't always. How often has the restaurant kitchen prepared your meal incorrectly? Or the airline lost your luggage? And doesn't it seem that the copying machine always breaks down thirty minutes after the repairman leaves?

Over the years, we've developed a 10-point mental checklist that helps us do a job right the first time. In a minute, I'll give you an example of how we applied the checklist to a new idea we were thinking of trying, so you can see how it works in practice; but here's the list.

1 *What's the benefit to the customer?*

2 *Will the customer easily understand that benefit?*

3 *What impact will this idea, program, or system have on our employees?*

4 *How will it affect our existing systems?*

5 *Is anybody else doing it successfully? What can we learn from their experience?*

6 *What could go wrong?*

7 *Will it give us an advantage over our competitors?*

8 *How much will it cost?*

9 *Will it make money?*

10 *When should we evaluate it?*

Before we change the way we do anything, we always ask these 10 questions. Before we go ahead, we must be comfortable with the answer to each one.

Here's how we used that list recently. Somebody suggested we should have express checkout in our service department, just as they do in hotels. We'd ask the customer for a credit card, when she dropped her car off for service; then, when we had completed the work, we'd fill out the charge slip, put the receipt in the glove compartment, lock up the car, and leave it out front so the customer could pick it up at her convenience.

The idea sounded good. Customers wouldn't have to wait on line to pay their bill, and, as I've said, they'd know in advance what the work would cost, because we give guaranteed estimates.

I liked the idea a lot when I first heard it, so we started applying our checklist to see if there were any potential problems I was missing.

1 *What's the benefit to the customer?* That seemed pretty clear. She would be able to get out of the dealership faster. This would remove another hassle for our customers.

2 *Will the customer easily understand that benefit?* This is important because customers will not take advantage of new ideas—no matter how great they are—if they're too hard to learn or understand.

We didn't seem to have that problem here. Once we said "express checkout," customers thought about the way they paid their hotel bills. And even people who don't stay in hotels a lot understood the concept pretty quickly, once we explained it to them.

3 *What impact will this idea have on our employees?* Minimal in this case. It meant a little bit more work for our service advisers. They'd have to take a credit card imprint when the customer dropped off the car, but since it

would mean less work for our cashiers—they would be helping fewer customers, once the program was in place—we considered this a wash.

4 *How will it affect our existing systems?* It wouldn't, really. The only major difference would be the way we delivered cars to the customer. Instead of a technician parking the car out in the back lot when he had finished whatever service work needed to be done, we'd park it around front.

5 *Is anybody else doing it? What can we learn from their experience?* I don't like to be a pioneer. Pioneers, as the old saying goes, are the people who get arrows in their backs. Wherever possible we like to borrow from others and learn from their mistakes, instead of making the mistakes ourselves. In this case, lots of hotels had express checkout. We modeled our system after theirs.

6 *What could go wrong?* A lot of things, but it turned out that none of the potential problems were insurmountable.

For one thing, the cars could be stolen. They would no longer be behind a locked gate. They'd be out in front, where it would be easier for the customer—and unfortunately a crook—to get them. But we figured if we left the cars where they were visible from the showroom we'd be okay, as long as the cars were locked.

But the idea of locking them brought up another problem. For the new system to work, customers needed to have two sets of keys to their automobile. We would lock the one they gave us inside their car when we had made the repair. That meant they'd need a second key set to get in. (Under our old system, we just handed them back their keys when they came to pick up the car.) We'd have to make sure they had those extra keys. If they didn't, it was no big deal. We could make them. We already had a key cutter. The only problem would be remembering to ask the customer if we should make her a spare.

But there was simply no way around the biggest problem: some people— not many, maybe a handful—didn't, to be blunt, trust us. They just didn't like the idea of giving us a credit card imprint before the work was done, even though they knew we couldn't charge them more than the estimate. They just hated the idea of our having their credit card number before the work was completed. There was nothing we could do to win those people over, so we stopped trying. But everyone else liked the idea.

7 *Will it give us an advantage over our competitors?* Yes. This was something the other guys didn't have. It would be another way we could stay ahead of them.

8 *How much will it cost?* Not much. We had to print cards that described the program, and we ordered some buttons that said: "Ask us about express checkout." The whole expense was maybe $500.

9 *Will it make money?* We feel that anything that makes life a little easier for the customer will make us more profitable. It gives the customer another reason to keep doing business with us.

10 *When should we evaluate it?* We decided to review the program monthly to see how it's doing. So far a lot of people like it.

There are a couple of other points to make about all this.

For one thing, "Do it right the first time" should start with the products we sell. We ought to be selling the best there is. The better the product, the less likely it is the customer will have a problem with it. (We'll spend some more time talking about that in Section VIII, *"Creating products that are easy to sell."*)

Second, a variation on the Golden Rule comes into play here: give people the kinds of things you'd like to have.

If the customer doesn't know the difference between product A and product B, we recommend the one we feel good about, the one that's best for him and his circumstances. We should do that even though we might make more money by selling him a brand with a higher margin.

When we sell a customer what we feel good about, he ends up with what he needs, which means we've done our job right.

CHECKLIST

✔ *Keep the service promise.* Doing what you're supposed to do, when you are supposed to do it, is the very minimum required to provide good customer service.

✔ *Sell the product you like the best.* If you only recommend the best product for the job, or only suggest the best way of going about it, your customer is bound to end up happier than if you try to cut a corner or sell him something he didn't need. The result is the customer is likely to come back.

✔ *You know you're on the right track* . . . when customers start expecting you to get it right every time. You want them to take that for granted.

When something goes wrong

What happens when something goes wrong?

Despite hiring the best people, constantly talking about the importance of doing the work right the first time, and all the systems we've put in place to ensure that nothing goes wrong, invariably something will. What do you do then?

It's an important question, because often the way our customers judge us is by the way we handle their problem. We're expected to do a good job—and people tend to take that for granted. What they really remember is what we did for them when something went wrong.

So what do we do?

First we apologize. Then we fix the problem.

Immediately.

Over the last twenty years, I've found those are the two keys to handling complaints.

First the apology.

We have to make a big deal out of being wrong. For one thing, we were wrong. The mistake should not have happened. And for another, the problem—no matter what it is—is a very big deal to the customer.

Let's suppose for a minute that we weren't in the car business but instead had a chain of blue jeans stores. We might be selling 1000 pairs a day, and know the odds say that 4 out of those 1000 will be defective somehow. That means every day when we come to work we know, on average, there will be 4 problems. That's 20 problems a week, 1000 in a year, and after a while we might start telling ourselves, "Hey, we're doing pretty well. For every 1000 we sell, 996 are fine."

The occasional defect may not seem like such a big deal to us. But it is to the customer. He's not buying 1,000 pairs of jeans, or 100 or even 10. He's buying one. And he doesn't want to hear, "Well, these things are to be expected," when he brings the defective one back to us. As far as he's concerned, we've screwed up 100% of the time—he bought one pair of jeans from us and that one pair was defective.

He doesn't want to hear about our 99.6% success rate, or how we don't get many customers complaining about our blue jeans. He has a problem, and he wants to know what we're going to do about it.

The first thing he must know is that we sincerely regret making the mistake.

Normally a spoken apology will be enough. But if it's a bigger deal, we might write a note, or call, or even—if the problem warrants it (the salesperson, for example, forgot to pick up the car for service)—send a dozen roses.

As a rule, the person who has the relationship with the customer (salesperson; service adviser) makes the apology. But for major sins, a manager will apologize, or I will. For example, if we wreck your car— and unfortunately, that does happen on occasion—*everyone* will apologize. (We will also repair or replace it.)

But whatever we do, the customer has to recognize that we're sincere. We don't have a preprinted apology form, designed to cover any problem, that we send out when something goes wrong. That's just about as bad as doing nothing at all. We respond in a way that assures the customer that we feel badly about causing him a problem. That, after all, is the way we *do* feel. We are in business to take care of our customers, not cause them problems.

Okay, saying we're sorry covers the first part of handling a complaint. But just apologizing isn't enough. We have to correct what went wrong. For example, here's how we handle a car that's been brought back to us because we didn't fix it right.

Immediately after we say we're sorry, we take the car into the shop, where it gets worked on first, no matter how many other automobiles we have waiting. And the technician who worked on the car initially will be the one who makes the repair.

But before he goes to work, his supervisors will talk to him. The fault may not lie with the technician. The service adviser might have given him the wrong instructions, or the part he installed may have failed after the customer got the car home. But no matter what caused the problem, everyone is going to make sure that he feels comfortable with what he's about to do.

We make a big deal out of our mistakes. And by making a big deal out of them—talking to the technician, the service adviser, and the shop managers—we all understand how important it is to do the job right the first time.

Nobody likes to hear they've done a lousy job, but criticism from customers is more valuable than praise. You want your customers to tell you when you've screwed up, so that you can take care of the problem and take steps to ensure it doesn't happen again—to them, or anybody else. If they don't tell you, they'll just walk away shaking their heads and they'll never come back. Worse, you're likely to alienate somebody else in the future by doing exactly the same thing.

There's a selfish reason for doing all this. It's more profitable, it reduces the amount of work we have to do over for free, and it decreases the stress factor with your customers.

One of my favorite parts of this job is running into somebody who tells me how wonderfully he was treated and how smoothly everything went.

My least favorite part of the job is listening to somebody tell me how we failed. Boy, I hate it when somebody says, "you think you have this wonderful reputation, well, let me tell you what you did to me." I just feel awful when that happens, and it doesn't matter how nicely somebody tries to tell me about the mistake.

But as much as I hate to hear criticism, I want customers to tell us when we've done a bad job. We have to know what we're doing wrong, in order to be able to set it right.

If we want people to tell us about our shortcomings, we have to make it easy for them.

Some people want to tell you face to face. They need to vent their feelings immediately. While they're describing their problem, we try not to interrupt—even if we know within a few words exactly what went wrong and how to fix it. We still need to let them tell us. It's almost like a catharsis for them.

But other people don't feel comfortable complaining that way. That's why we have that three-question form at the cashier's window, all the other customer surveys we use, and the focus groups.

We want the customer to tell us what we're doing wrong. If they're unhappy and don't tell us, eventually they're going to stop doing business with us. However, every customer service study ever done shows that if we fix the problem, or at the very least say we're sorry about what went wrong, we have a very good chance of holding on to their business.

So, no matter how uncomfortable it is for us, we have to find out what we did wrong. Unfortunately, that's the only way we're going to be able to do a better job of getting it right in the future.

There's one other point to make about mistakes. When you set high standards for yourself, some people are going to start looking for you to fail. They'll search to find a gum wrapper in the parking lot, or for someone who might not have been as nice to them as they should have been. They'll be waiting for you to stub your toe.

That's okay. It just gives you another reason to avoid mistakes and keep getting better.

CHECKLIST

✔ *When something goes wrong . . .* and it will, no matter how hard you try, apologize. It's easy, customers like it, but almost no one ever says they're sorry. Then, immediately after you apologize, fix the problem while the customer is still there.

✔ *Make it easy for customers to complain.* It's unpleasant, but at least you'll have a chance to set things right.

✔ *You want people to hold your feet to the fire.* By setting high standards for yourself, you'll encourage a certain percentage of people to seek out every potential flaw. Good. It gives you another reason to eliminate those flaws.

✔ *Everybody has a bad day.* Even customers. If they lose their temper, forgive them. Go out of your way to make them feel comfortable about coming back. (They might be a little embarrassed.)

CHAPTER 10

How to have what your customers want

As we said earlier, one of the best ways of providing service is to ask the customer what he wants and then give it to him.

But how can you give the customer what he wants if you don't have it?

You can't.

And that gets us to the importance of inventory, and a system for handling it.

One way to ensure that the customer is never disappointed is always to have a huge inventory on hand. That's an option, of course, but a very expensive one. Carrying all that inventory costs money, and too much inventory, and not enough sales, is a surefire way of going broke.

A better way of always having what the customer wants is to have a system that analyzes your inventory and lets you know what you should have in stock and what you shouldn't. That system should also measure your cost of capital (on our $20 million worth of new car, used car, and parts inventory the interest—at 9.75% annually—costs us $1.95 million a year).

For example, here's how we track new car inventory. We want 45 days' worth of cars on the ground, and that's a number that's been steadily shrinking. Traditional factory guidelines call for dealers having inventories of 60 to 90 days, but as prices of cars have climbed—increasing our interest expense—we've reduced our inventory. It's now down to 45 days, and it will get lower as manufacturers learn how to shorten the time between order and delivery. Today, it takes approximately six weeks for us to get a car, but Cadillac's manufacturing guru Gary Cowger has pledged to get it down to two weeks.

We balance our inventory across all models—we want 45 days' supply of Coupe de Villes, 45 days' of Fleetwoods, etc.—that way, if we get short in one, or long in another, we know what to order and what *not* to.

Looking at sales by specific product line (Eldorado), as opposed to total sales (all Cadillacs), allows us to reorder the best-sellers, even if total sales are slow (as they always are after a rebate program ends). There's a temptation not to order anything when things are not going well. But if you do that you could be cutting off your nose to spite your face.

We also track our inventory by age. If a car has been sitting on the lot for more than 45 days, there's a reason it hasn't sold. There's probably something wrong with it. It may be an unpopular color, or it's dirty and parked in the corner. We need to go look at it and find out what's the matter. It's just as important to find out why something isn't selling as why it is.

But the most important thing we measure is availability, i.e., how often do we have in stock what the customer wants? If a customer asks for something we don't have, we record his request as a lost sale. We track lost sales closely. It's another way to help us figure out what to order. Too often, department store buyers tend to rely on instinct, and instinct alone is not enough. You need to know *exactly* what the customer wants.

If a customer asks for something you don't have, try to get it by calling a competitor and working out a trade. As long as the arrangement is reciprocal, your competition is likely to agree.

How much inventory we have on hand is determined by how fast the item sells, how long it takes to restock it, and interest carrying costs. Obviously, the faster the order-to-delivery cycle, the less we need in inventory. For example, if we are using 200 of something a week—like oil filters—why would we want a 45 days' supply on hand? That's an awful lot of money tied up in inventory. Since we know that we use 200 filters a week, we might keep 400 in stock, and then order replacements weekly.

Lexus has the best automobile parts inventory management system in the world. It allows us to reorder what we need daily. This means higher availability and lower inventory costs for us—and them.

To figure out how long date-sensitive inventory has been sitting on the shelf, we use color-coded tags. Every piece of merchandise has one, and the color of the tag tells us how long we've had a part sitting around. A blue tag means the part came in January, red February. You get the idea.

If you're in a retail business, like clothing, where people see your inventory because it's out on the floor, you can be more subtle. A large triangle on the price tag could mean the merchandise arrived in March. A very visible square would indicate it came in April. (We use color-coded dots, which we place on the back of the car's rear-view mirror.)

All these ideas will help limit inventory and decrease overhead. But even with the world's best inventory control system, you're not always going to have what a customer asks for.

One way to expand your inventory for free is to establish trading relationships with people in similar businesses. Say you run a woman's clothing store. You should be able to trade with other nearby stores to get things your customers want. Maybe black is a hot color for you and green is hot for them, or maybe their supplier didn't ship him any greens. You can trade.

In our case, we trade with other car dealers all the time, even competitors. And if a customer has his heart set on a particular car, say one that has a unique color combination, we'll go to just about any length to get it. We have traded with car dealers as far away as Seattle.

The ability to swap merchandise lets you expand your available inventory without actually having to carry it. We've found it's a very useful idea.

CHECKLIST

✔ *Is it in stock? Should it be? How long has it been there? How many should we have?* If your inventory system can't answer these questions, you're making your job of providing good customer service a lot harder than it has to be.

✔ *What's your inventory costing you?* By carefully monitoring what's on hand, you'll be able to turn your merchandise faster, which will reduce your carrying costs.

✔ *Measure your order-to-delivery cycle for each supplier*, and work toward having a "just in time" inventory system.

✔ *Establish trading partners.* You don't want a potential customer to leave just because you don't have what he wants in stock. Work out relationships with nearby businesses so that you can swap merchandise as the situation arises.

CHAPTER 11

Good enough never is

We were the first automobile dealer in Texas to provide free loan cars for service customers and to be open all day Saturday for service. These ideas gave us a tremendous advantage over our competitors—for several years. The problem was, the lead didn't last. Our two largest competitors eventually copied what we did. Today, they now have the second and third largest loan car fleets in the country. (They each have about 50 cars. We have a total of 257.) And they, too, now offer Saturday service.

So we decided to raise the ante. We extended our service hours until 8 P.M., so that no one had to break his neck to get to our dealership before the service department closed at six.

Again we were copied.

So again we raised the stakes.

We got secretaries for our Cadillac and Lexus salespeople so we could take the loan car to the customer. The secretary drops off the loaner and drives the customer's car back to our shop. When we finish the service work, he or she drives the car back and picks up the loaner. The customer never has to come in at all.

Where will these improvements to our service program end? They won't. If we want to attract more customers—and keep the ones we have—we need to keep giving them more reasons to do business with us.

We have to keep adding new ideas and improving the ones we have, because consumers don't give us a whole lot of points for being first. If somebody offers them more—more convenience, more service, or a much better price—they're going to leave, no matter what we've done for them in the past.

That means we must set high standards for ourselves and constantly exceed them. We have to because Satchel Paige got it wrong.

Paige was a great pitcher who played baseball until he was in his fifties—or maybe older. Nobody ever did figure out his real age. And toward the end of his career he was asked for the secret of his long and healthy life.

"Why," a reporter wanted to know, "were you able to pitch for so many years?"

"I owe it all to doing everything in moderation and avoiding fried or fatty foods," Paige replied.

"Is there any advice you'd like to pass on to others?" the reporter asked.

"Yes," said Paige. "Don't ever look back, because something might be gaining on you."

That's a great story. But we better be looking backward, forward, and all around. Because as the examples of our competitors extending their service hours and creating a loan car fleet show, people *are* gaining on us—constantly. It's become a cliché by now, but it really is true: if you're not getting better you're getting worse. The Japanese call the process of continuous improvement *kaizen*. It doesn't matter what you call it, as long as you do it. Getting better—continuously—is absolutely necessary if you're going to survive.

There are numerous ways we try to improve ourselves.

For one thing, we shop our competitors. We're always checking to see if they've instituted a new program that we should copy. And we also want to know how they are selling against us. For example, when we first started offering loaner cars, here's what they'd say if a customer asked why Sewell provided them and they didn't.

"Yes," our competitors said, "Sewell Village *says* they offer loaners. But did you ever try to get one? If you call up, they'll tell you you'll have to wait a month before one's available."

Now that wasn't true. But we often had a waiting list.

We were going to add more cars to our loan car fleet anyway, but once we knew what the competition was saying about us, we made it a top priority.

In addition to shopping our competitors, we borrowed an idea from restaurants and department stores: we shop ourselves. We hire a firm that twice a year sends people in to buy a car from us. We don't know who the person is or when he or she is coming.

When the person comes in he checks a list of things we've asked the mystery shopping firm to grade us on. Did we greet the "customer" quickly? Did the salesperson take him for a test drive? Did we follow up with him? After the visit, the firm gives us a full report. Mystery shoppers are another way to find areas where we can improve.

We have to do these sorts of things to stay ahead. It's just like sports.

World championship teams that stand pat rarely repeat for a second, third or fourth year. Maybe they get complacent. Maybe their players get older and can't perform quite as well. Maybe it's because the other teams keep making trades and drafting players to improve themselves. But whatever the reason, dynasties are hard to come by.

That's also true in business. The level of competition is rising every single day—for example, all the car buff magazines have said that Lexus has set a new standard for luxury cars, one that all the other automobile manufacturers will now have to match—so you need to keep getting better. The most important system you can put in place is one that demands continuous improvements.

Set high goals and keep raising them once they're achieved. If you don't, somebody will blow right by you while you're telling yourself what a great job you've done. Good enough never is.

How do we implement a continuous improvement program? It's not hard, just time-consuming. Periodically we examine every single part of our operation and see how it can be improved. We don't do it all at once. Maybe every March and September, we look at our landscaping. In February and August we make it a point to look at our furniture and showrooms to see what is beginning to look dated or worn. The exact timetable is flexible. The important thing is to do the reviews at fixed intervals.

We apply the same review process to our systems. Periodically we'll look at something like our hiring processes, to see where we can improve. We don't go into the review thinking we have to scrap what we're doing. We're just looking for ways to make it better.

For example, our salespeople had been selling 16 cars a month. That's not too bad—it's twice the national average—but during a recent review we tried to figure out a way to improve that a bit. We created an incentive program, Team 20, which rewards a salesperson for selling 20 or more cars in a month. The more cars they sell, the more free travel, luggage, or cash they'll receive.

In service, our CSI rating is now 96%; by rereading Deming and Taguchi, we're looking for ways to get it up to 98% within a year.

We always aim for total success. We want the best salespeople and

100% CSI. But, realistically, we know we can't make huge changes overnight. We make small improvements, but we make them continuously.

This process never ends. If our CSI is 96% and we get up to 98%, the natural tendency is to throw a party and then relax a bit. After all, it took a lot of effort to record that improvement. But while we should celebrate our successes (*see Chapter 12*), we can't celebrate for too long.

If we do, we might find that somebody is not only gaining on us, they've zipped right by while we were patting ourselves on the back.

CHECKLIST

✔ *Being first is not good enough.* Neither Pepsi nor Coke invented diet colas or sodas without caffeine. The innovations came from others, yet Coke and Pepsi now own the market. If you stop once you have a new idea, you're in trouble.

✔ *Make it better.* Once you have improved an idea, do it again. If you want to stay ahead of the pack, there must be *continuous* improvement —everywhere within your company.

✔ *Periodically review every part of your operation.* This will make it easy for you to find things that can be improved.

✔ *Skulduggery* . . . is good. You should periodically shop your competition and yourself, looking for places where you can improve.

THREE

People: how to care for customers—and employees

CHAPTER 12

Q: Who's more important?
Your customer or your employee?
A: Both

This is a good place to say what has been implied all along: our people are just as important as our customers, and they need to be treated just as well.

Why? For one thing, it's the right thing to do. For another, it's in our self-interest. How can we expect our people to be good to our customers if we're treating *them* badly?

There are some people who'll ask: "Why do I have to bother? I'm paying them, aren't I? Isn't that enough?"

Hell, no.

As we've said, pay is not the primary reason people give when they're asked to explain why they do—or don't—like their jobs. Long before they get around to talking about money, they'll say things like, "It's a nice place to work," "They really care about what happens to me," or, "They treat me like an adult."

Treating your employees well starts with their work area. Not many people get to see our service repair shop—our insurance company wants to keep traffic there to a minimum—but those who do always comment on its cleanliness. And, in fact, it's immaculate.

Why? Because, while customers rarely see it, our technicians do. They live and work there every day. Where would you like to spend your day, in a place that's dirty or one that's spotless?

But it's more than just aesthetics. If we make the technicians' work environment more professional, more pleasant, more efficient, if we provide them with the very best equipment and tools, we're going to be able to hire the best technicians.

The professional technicians you need to work on today's cars are virtually engineers. Some of the guys working in our service department never went to college, for one reason or another, but they all have the mental ability to be engineers. People who are that bright don't want to spend all day in a dark, greasy pit. They want a pleasant environment, just as we all do. So we provide them with one. In addition to being clean, it's safe and well lit. All this gives them another reason for working for us instead of our competition.

For our salespeople, we make sure they have their own individual office area, where they can display pictures of their families or hobbies, instead of putting everyone in one big room known not so affectionately as a bullpen.

This just makes sense. How can you expect a salesperson to be a professional if he has to share a desk or work within a four-foot by four-foot space with movable walls?

We always try to thank our customers for doing business with us, and we always try to thank our employees for doing a good job. Both those thank yous are equally important.

I think we're also able to attract better people because of the way we treat them. We really want to create a family atmosphere. Each general manager has a list of doctors, hospitals, lawyers, and accountants they can refer employees to if they need help.

And just as we thank our customers for doing business with us, we thank our employees for doing a good job. That's a big deal.

We say thank you in a lot of ways. When someone goes out of his way for a customer, we write about it in the *100% Newsletter*, our internal publication. That reinforces what they did, and it's another way of communicating our values to everyone who works here.

We've also created the "Pat on the Back" award. We tell everybody who works here, if they catch somebody doing something right—someone who has really extended himself for a customer—to write down what he saw on the "Pat on the Back" form and give it to the employee who went "above and beyond the call of duty." It's a three-part form. The employee who did the outstanding job gets the top copy, the middle one goes to the employee's manager, and a copy goes to me. It's a fun idea and people like to know that someone noticed their good deed.

Barbecues are one of our favorite ways to celebrate our successes and show our thanks. When we achieve a record Customer Service Index we have a barbecue. We hang banners all over the place, everybody shows up, we talk about what a good job they've done. We always hold those picnics on company time. (People come and go in shifts so we can continue to take care of our customers.)

Holding these celebrations during the workday is another way to say thank you.

CHECKLIST

✔ *Have you thanked your employees today?* If you thank your customers, you should also thank the folks who do the work.

✔ *There are lots of things you can delegate* . . . but thanking people for doing a good job isn't one of them. Thank yous mean more coming from the boss—merely because he is the boss.

✔ *Whenever possible, show your gratitude on company time.* If you are going to throw a party to say thanks, why not have it begin at 3 P.M. on a Wednesday instead of Sunday at two? It shows people you are serious about your appreciation.

✔ *Create "110% awards"* . . . *and hand them out often.* Plaques, pictures, and pins really work.

CHAPTER 13

The customer *isn't* always right

You've heard the old saying a thousand times: the customer is always right. And I think that's true.

Most of the time.

If the customer is unhappy with something we've done, we'll ask him what's wrong and fix it for free. Almost always.

But is the customer always and absolutely right no matter what?

No.

What causes the exceptions? Often it is a question of fairness, and sometimes the amount of money involved can also make a difference.

When the amounts are small, the customer *is* always right. Stew Leonard, who runs the world's largest dairy store, tells a wonderful story about a woman who bought two pounds of filet mignon from him when he was selling filets for $5.98 a pound. The next week he put steaks on sale and filet mignon cost $4.98 a pound. The woman came back in and demanded that he give her the $2 she would have saved if she had waited a week.

He gave her the $2. And I would have too.

But $2,000? That's a different matter, isn't it?

When people tell stories about the customer always being right, the amount of money involved is always pretty small. We hear about Stew Leonard, or maybe McDonald's, where they'll automatically replace your order if you're unhappy, but the stories always involve inexpensive products.

Up to $500, we're probably not going to argue with anybody. But beyond that it gets into a judgment area.

Let me give you a couple of examples.

There was a man who brought in his car for service and left in the trunk a bag of quail he had shot. He says, "I told my service adviser, Rusty, he could have the quail."

Rusty says: "He never mentioned the quail to me. I knew the car was going to be here for two weeks while the customer went on vacation. If I had known there were quail in it, I would have known enough to get them out."

Now during those two weeks the quail fermented and exploded, and the overpowering smell permeated the entire car. While we were able to pick up the pieces, the quail odor wouldn't come out, no matter what we did.

If you want to keep their business, give customers exactly what they ask for—or even more—without any hesitation. If you do anything less, you might as well offer them nothing, because you'll have lost their good will.

There was no doubt in my mind that the customer was wrong, that he never said anything about the quail being there. But because he was convinced he was right, and he had been doing business with us for a long time, we bought the car back from him. (We sold it to a wholesaler—a used car broker who sells only to other dealers—who thought he had a way to take care of the problem.)

It's okay—up to a certain point—to let a customer take advantage of you. And that happens upon occasion. Not often, fortunately. Virtually all of our customers are as wonderful as they can be. But it does happen. For instance:

∗ *A customer claims he left a tennis racquet in the car when he dropped it off for service, and now it's not there. I know our service guys are really not into tennis; still, we bought him another racquet.*

∗ *I remember about fifteen years ago, when Gant shirts were $6.50, a stockbroker said he had been in and torn his Gant shirt on something, and he sent us a bill for $65. We paid it.*

(There was a guy who did something like that nationally. He wrote to lots of dealerships saying he ripped a shirt while he was looking at a car, adding that people in the dealership were very rude to him when he mentioned it. He went on to say how he knew the dealer really wouldn't condone such a thing, and while it was no big deal, the shirt cost $35, and he thought the owner would like to know what happened. He mailed that letter to every Cadillac dealer in the country, and he made a bunch of money by taking advantage of the dealers' desire to please their customers.)

* Then there are the customers who say the coins they keep to pay tolls for the highway were stolen, or a new sports jacket is missing from the trunk, or that the grease on our driveway ruined a new pair of shoes. In each case, we write them a check.*

It's the cost of doing business, and we budget accordingly.

Can we get cheated?

Yes.

Do we mind getting cheated a little bit?

No.

There is a percentage of people in the world who are just made like that. They feel they win if they take advantage of us.

We can get cynical over time, but we have to fight against it because 99% of the people are just as honest as they can be. They truly believe the tennis racquet was in the trunk when they left the car off for service, even though they made five stops before they saw us, a couple afterward, and didn't realize the racquet was missing until they got home.

If we start trying to figure out who's lying to us, invariably we'll guess wrong and alienate a good customer. We're far better off assuming that if a customer tells us he has a problem he really does have a problem.

In dealing with an unhappy customer, the question becomes: what really is the right thing to do?

In *Minding the Store*, Stanley Marcus said if you want to keep their business, give customers all of what they ask for, without equivocation or quibble. If you bargain with them, you're going to lose their good will.

If you tell us the shirt you ripped cost $100, and we say, "We're awfully sorry," and write you a check for $100, then everything is fine.

But if the customer says it's a $100 shirt, and we say, "You know, you've had that shirt for a little while. There's probably some depreciation, so why don't we give you $50?" then there's trouble. If we pay $50, we might as well have done nothing, because we've lost the customer's good will by arguing over what the shirt was worth.

Stanley tells a wonderful story that happened when he first started working at the store. A woman bought a ball gown fashioned of handmade lace. She took it home, wore it once and, in Stanley's words, "clearly abused it; it looked like she had wrestled in it." Then she brought it back to Neiman-Marcus and said she wanted her money back.

Stanley gave it to her—cheerfully—reasoning that it would cost a lot more to replace that customer than the $175 (remember this was 1932) the dress would cost him. He was right. "Over the years," Stanley writes, "this woman spent $500,000 with us."

Once I read that in Stanley's book, it made my life a lot easier. Instead of getting uptight about what is a fair deal, we, like Stanley Marcus, take a longer-term view of the value of a customer.

If the amount is less than $500, the department manager has the authority to make the adjustment. Anything larger should be approved by the general manager. The goal should always be to do whatever it takes to keep the customer coming back.

Now, when someone is trying to take *extreme* advantage of you, then you have to evaluate whether it's worth it.

If a customer buys a car from us, takes it home, and shows it to her husband, who says, "I hate green. I really wanted blue, take it back," we will exchange the green car for a blue one.

But if she buys a car from us, and then ten days later finds out she could have bought the car for $250 less someplace else, the answer is going to be no. She can't bring it back. She made a deal, and that's the deal we're going to stick with.

Every once in a while you come across a customer who is just impossible. Maybe it's a man who sexually harasses a saleswoman, or is constantly abusive to our employees, or finds fault with absolutely everything we do. In those kinds of cases we have to say, "we're sorry, but maybe you'd be happier doing business somewhere else." It takes a lot to get me to that point—it happens about once a year—but when I reach it, I have no problem suggesting that they buy somewhere else.

Sometimes we even give them directions to our "favorite" competitor.

CHECKLIST

✔ *The customer* is *always right—up to a point.* Your job is to figure out what that point is. We stretch pretty far to decide in the customer's favor. You should too. It's profitable.

✔ *Be taken advantage of with a smile.* If you've decided to give the customer what he wants, give in completely and cheerfully. Don't haggle over the amount, and don't roll your eyes or be sarcastic. If you are anything less than cheerful, it will cost you all the good will you were trying to gain.

✔ *Customers are good.* If a customer tells you he has a problem, the chances are 99 out of a 100 he really does. Don't let the other 1% make you mistreat everyone else.

CHAPTER 14

How to teach customers
to get the best service

Providing good service doesn't have to be a one-way street. You can teach customers how to get better service.

We start by having them help us even out our work flow.

Think about what happens every time you want to get something repaired. You're almost always told: "No problem, but be sure to bring it in here first thing tomorrow." That's not good for anybody. *Everyone* shows up at seven-thirty, or whenever the doors open, there's a long line, and everybody ends up being miserable. The customer has to wait for someone to take care of him, and the service department gets frustrated because they're overwhelmed.

That's no way to provide good service, so we handle things a bit differently.

Let's say a customer calls, wanting to bring his car in. Like everyone else, we'll say no problem, but then we'll look at the appointments we have already scheduled. If it looks like seven-thirty is going to be a real busy time, we'll ask if the customer can drop his car off in the afternoon. Nine times out of ten, he'll say yes. If that's no good, we'll ask, "how about lunchtime, or on your way home?" (Remember, we're going to give him a free loaner to use while his is in the shop.)

By providing a list of alternative times, we're trying to make the drop-off as easy as possible for the customer. Plus, it's helping us, because we end up writing the work up at lunchtime, or the end of the day, when we normally don't have a lot of customers coming in. Heck, if he brings the car in at 5 P.M. we may get part of the job done before the technician goes home; plus, the technician will have the car there waiting for him when he comes to work the next day. He might even come in early to work on it.

Not everybody has to bring the car in first thing, and that's a good thing because, by spreading the work out, we have more time to spend with each customer learning in detail what needs to be repaired.

It's a whole lot harder to do a repair right, or to provide good service, if you don't know what needs to be fixed or what the customer wants. Find ways to get your customers to spend an extra ten minutes to describe in detail what needs to be repaired or what they want you to do. It will be time well spent for both of you.

One of the few problems we have with customers is getting them to spend enough time with us to discuss what's wrong. If you'll let us, we'll spend a lot of time talking to you about what's wrong, because it increases our chances of fixing it right.

For example, we are more than happy to pick up a customer's car when it's time for routine maintenance work, like an oil change. But we recommend that a customer bring the car to us personally if it has one of those nagging wind noises or rattles. That way they can show us exactly where it makes the noise. It's just like going to the doctor. If he has a chance to examine you, and you really explain what's wrong, he can be more effective than if you just have him prescribe medicine over the phone.

Customers are always in a hurry, but we tell them that if they'll just spend an extra ten minutes explaining what's wrong, our chances of fixing it are at least doubled. When we put it that way, customers are willing to take the time. Nobody—not us, and certainly not the customer—wants the work to come back a second time for the same repair. (And if they're not bringing the car in first thing in the morning—when we could be swamped with customers and they're worried about being late to work—then we both have the time to spend to ensure that the job will be done right the first time.)

Most often spending that extra time up front will help save some time in the future. We try to get customers to tell us what their special wants and desires are. Do you want us to wash the car each time you bring it in? You prefer 10-40 oil? You like Michelin tires? Fine. We make a note of those things, and hopefully we'll never have to ask again.

There's one other way we show customers how to get good service. That's by being nice to them. If we're nice to them, they'll almost always be nice in return. They'll be more patient with us, and that makes it easier for us to get the work done. It's hard to do a good job with customers screaming at you.

We also try to make it easier for customers to deal with us by explaining how we do things. For example, we tell customers that the first thing we always do, when they come in, is pull the chart that has their car's service history on it. That record also tells us who their service adviser is. (Customers deal with the same one each time, so we can build a relationship with them. We want them to feel comfortable doing business with us, and building individual relationships helps us do that. When he hears a strange noise under the hood, we hope the customer says: "I don't know what's causing that rattle; I'll take it to my [personal service] adviser Alan and he'll take care of it for me.")

Once we know who the service adviser is, we put a little numbered, color-coded tag on top of the car that identifies him as Alan's customer and shows when he arrived. Alan can then look out across the sea of cars and find the next car he should deal with.

Since the customer knows how the system works, when he sees us rushing around working on other people's cars, he doesn't feel that we've forgotten about him. He knows it's just like the bakery on Sunday morning. Everyone has a number and will be called in order, so there's no need to worry about somebody being served out of turn.

The customer is happy, and it is easier to get the work done.

CHECKLIST

✔ *Let the customers help you provide good service.* Teach them how to get the best service; when it's a good time to come see you; and what they need to tell you in order to get the job done right the first time.

✔ *If you smile, odds are they'll smile back.* If you are polite, the customers probably will be polite in return. That makes it a lot easier to get the work done right.

✔ *Explain to customers how you do things.* You may have the world's best system for getting things done, but if the customers don't understand it, they're likely to be confused at best—and angry at worst. Once they understand you have systems—and that those systems work—they're bound to think better of you and want to come back.

CHAPTER 15

Creating frequent buyers

The employees at American Airlines may call Chairman Bob Crandall "Darth Vader," but he sure is smart. If ever there was any doubt—and I am not sure that there ever was—American's creation of the airline industry's first frequent flyer program proved that.

Frequent flyer programs underscore just how important the airlines think their customers are. Every business should have this kind of program. It's another way of creating customer loyalty. We want people to come back and do business with us again and again. That's the whole idea behind providing excellent customer service.

If we can get the customer to come back, look what happens:

First, our sales go up. The customer is buying more from us.

Second, we strengthen our position in the marketplace. If the customer is buying from us, he's not shopping at the competition.

Third, we cut our marketing costs. We don't have to spend as much money to attract that repeat customer. We already have him. And our marketing costs are reduced even further by the fact that our satisfied customers will tell their friends about how they like doing business with us—and, as we all know, there's no stronger form of advertising than word of mouth.

Fourth, it insulates us from price competition, because a loyal customer is less likely to be lured away by a discount of a few dollars.

Finally, a satisfied customer is likely to sample our other product lines. Because we've done a good job for him in the past, he's more likely to try another one of our products in the future.

Given all these advantages, I'd be hard pressed to think of a reason why you shouldn't have a frequent buyer program, modeled after what the airlines have done. For one thing, the mere existence of the program tells customers they're important. We know they are, but sometimes we

*F*requent *buyer programs prove to customers how important you think they are. By having one, you go beyond saying (an often mechanical) thank you. You actually reward people for doing business with you.*

forget to tell them. The last thing in the world we want to do is take a loyal customer for granted. This type of program shows we don't.

And there are a couple of more subtle points that are equally important. For one thing, the airlines do all the paperwork. Customers don't have to keep track of anything.

I think there is something a little bit degrading about forcing the customer to keep track of how much he has spent with you. A lot of businesses that reward customers require them to turn in receipts, or present a little card that's punched each time they buy something. I think it's wrong to ask customers to keep track of what they bought. It's almost like asking them to beg to get a present.

The frequent buyer programs also force the store owner to figure out who his best customers are. We may have a general idea that Ms. Jones has spent a lot of money with us over the years, but is she a better customer than Mr. Smith or Mrs. White? Nobody is smart enough to remember all that. But shouldn't we have that information?

My two favorite stories about that concern the Mansion hotel here in Dallas. When the owners got around to figuring out who their best customers were, they found that a couple of investment bankers were spending $20,000 *a month* in their restaurant. In their restaurant! All of a sudden they decided they owed those guys more than just a thank you.

A similar thing, on a much smaller scale, happened to me. We had held two "thank you" dinners for our salespeople at the Mansion, and one weekend my wife and I decided we wanted to get away from everybody. So I called to get us a room, and when we got there they had upgraded us to a suite. They recognized we were good customers, and they wanted to say thanks. It was a gesture we appreciated—and remembered.

We thank our customers in any number of ways: In person, on the phone (we always call a couple of days after someone buys a car from us, to make sure everything is okay, and to say, again, that we appreciate their business), and we send thank you notes to customers as a matter of course. We are also talking about sending people a beautiful Steuben bowl, after they've bought their twenty-fifth car from us. (I wonder how much you have to pay a lawyer, or a banker, before you get a thank you note, let alone a Steuben bowl.)

The reward program doesn't have to be tied to a specific purchase, however. For example, we have an annual party for our customers. One year it was an art show; another we had a Neiman-Marcus fashion show; we've also had Paul Prudhomme come and cook.

We have a list of everyone who has bought a car from us, and we invite them all to be our guests. We don't invite people whom we'd like to be our customers—although an individual salesman can do that if he wants. We limit the invitations to people who've done business with us in the past. We're not looking to drum up new customers; this is our way of saying thank you to the customers we already have.

It's also another way of maintaining our relationship with the customer, another chance for us to do something for him.

Some people will say reward programs are a waste of money. Their argument is since the frequent flyer, or the frequent buyer, is going to do business with you anyway, it's silly to reward him. All you're doing is taking money out of your pocket.

But how much money went into your pocket because of those good customers? Shouldn't you thank them for it?

And in a less altruistic way of thinking about all this, shouldn't you keep giving them reasons to keep doing business with you?

People like to be thanked for their business.

CHECKLIST

✔ *Stay in touch.* Once you have identified your best customers, communicate with them regularly. Maybe you send them a newsletter or invite them to a party. But between purchases, show they're not forgotten.

✔ *How often should you say thank you?* Every time you get a chance.

✔ *Blow your own horn—subtly.* Every time you correspond with a customer, include something along with the letter. It could be the description of a new product or service or the fact that you've extended your hours or have scheduled a sale.

CHAPTER 16

Making sure
you have the best people

Providing great customer service requires great people. I don't believe you can run an above-average business with average employees. To be the best, we need to find people who are 10s on a scale of 1 to 10.

We can wait for 10s to walk through the door, but that's not particularly efficient. After all, people are distributed evenly along a bell-shaped curve, so we'd end up spending a lot of time interviewing nine folks who don't qualify, before we find the one we want.

We try to short-circuit this problem by extensively interviewing people who apply for a job and then testing everyone who impresses us during the interviews. (We'll talk about testing in a minute.)

We have to devote this kind of attention to hiring. Our whole system of customer service depends on each customer having a good experience, no matter who they come in contact with. If they're going to have a good experience, we have to hire good people. In order to find them, we have to spend a lot of time interviewing.

While that sounds simple, the problem is, we get busy. And if four people apply for a job, we often try to convince ourselves that we should hire one of them, because those four people are probably as good as it gets.

If people have performed well in the past, they'll probably perform well in the future. So, in interviewing, look for people who have been successful and leaders.

But we know that's not true. Maybe the perfect person for the job is in that group of four, but the odds say he or she isn't. We probably need to interview twenty-five people to find a really good person, and we might have to interview a hundred folks to find someone who's truly exceptional. But who has that kind of time? At some point you have to stop interviewing.

Still, my feeling is, if you haven't talked to twenty-five people, you haven't looked hard enough.

Over the years we've figured out a pretty good way to identify exceptional people.

For one thing, we almost never advertise. The people we really want—the best people—already have jobs. They're not searching the help wanted ads or updating their résumés. In fact, most of the successful people we've hired have never had a résumé. *We* sought *them* out, because we had heard about the job they were doing somewhere else, or, as happens most often, they were referred by a friend. As a rule, people who are exceptional performers are friends with people who are exceptional performers, so we pay a lot of attention when one of our people recommends a friend.

There is another reason, though, why I'm not too keen on résumés. I think just sending in a résumé along with a cover letter when you are looking for a job shows a lack of aggressiveness and/or self-confidence. If a person doesn't believe in himself enough to come down to the dealership and schedule an appointment with us in person, I think he has said an awful lot about himself.

When the person does come in for an interview, we look for five specific qualities.

1 *History of success.* We want to hire people who have proven they're capable of getting things done. Their past successes don't necessarily have to be in our field, but we want to know: have they been successful in their other jobs? Their hobbies? In life? Have they had leadership positions?

If they've performed well in the past, they'll probably perform well in the future.

2 *Intelligence.* The testing we do will quantify this for us. Everything else being equal, bright people will do better—plus, they're more fun to be around. In our company that's particularly important because over time we've ended up with a group of very bright people, and they find it hard to work with someone who is not as quick as they are.

3 *Energy.* I like people who fidget and move around a lot during the interview. Often, it's not a sign of nervousness but rather an indication that they would rather be getting something accomplished, instead of sitting in a chair.

You can tell a lot about people's energy level if you ask about their hobbies. Do they hike, run, ski, play racquetball, or do they play chess, bridge, and read? (Ideally, they have both kinds of hobbies.)

Many of our people are ex-athletes. If you're a former jock, you probably have the durability to stand up to the hours we put in here—twelve-hour days are not uncommon—and the resilience to bounce back from criticism or losing a sale.

4 *Character.* We always do a credit and reference check and require a medical exam, which includes a drug test. (One out of three fails.) We want to operate a drug-free environment.

But we try to find out more. In talking with applicants, we try to discover if they truly like to help people. We also try to find out if they take pride in themselves and what they do. For example, we ask about the awards they've won. Their answers tell us not only that they're good at what they do but that they have enough pride to compete.

In addition, we want to get a sense of whether they follow through on things. For example, I always ask why an accountant has never taken the CPA exam, or how come a person who started college, or graduate school, never finished.

5 *Will they fit?* Clearly, this is an intangible, but an important one.

Take our salespeople. In addition to being aggressive, they tend to be thick-skinned, yet take losing a sale very personally. Most are athletic—and engage in what is euphemistically described as locker room humor. If you're sensitive, they'll torture the living bejesus out of you. As our first sales manager Ken Batchelor said: "If you've got any skeletons in your closet, you'd better come out bragging about them."

Here's an example. One of our very best salesmen, Tommy Armstrong, has a glass eye (the result of a childhood blasting cap). He's affectionately known as "Deadeye." Subtle.

If you're going to spend ten or twelve hours a day working with a group of people, it's a lot easier if you fit.

Having identified people we think would be good candidates, we send them out to be tested.

We've been testing people for fifteen years now. It started when we were approached by a well-respected local psychological testing firm, who told us that our hiring process would become more efficient if we tested everyone who applied for a job.

Since I grew up on a used car lot, I tend to be more skeptical than most people, so I decided to test the testers. I asked the firm to test all our current salespeople and rank them. Surprisingly, they identified the best performers, the ones who were average, and the people who could use some help.

I was impressed, and became even more so when Dr. Ron Trego, who has administered our tests all these years, suggested that we use the test results of our four top salespeople as a template for deciding whom we should hire in the future. That was an intriguing concept: test the best performers and try to hire more people like them. That strategy has worked for the last fifteen years. (A copy of one person's test results can be seen on page 71.)

It's like what happened when Lawrence Taylor came into the National Football League and began tearing up the place. Everybody said he would be the prototype for all future NFL linebackers. So what you have seen since is that everybody tries to draft linebackers who are just like Taylor: real big, real strong, real fast. Our prototypes are modeled on our best performers. They're our Lawrence Taylors.

Do tests always work? No. Do people with reading disabilities or folks who did not grow up with English as their first language have problems testing well? Sometimes. And no matter what the testing people say about their examinations not being culturally biased, I tend to discount the test results of a black or Hispanic who doesn't score well and place a lot more emphasis on her job history.

But on the whole testing makes sense. If we're going to hire a technician, why not hire someone with high mechanical aptitude, instead of someone like me whose mechanical skills are average at best? And we'd probably do even better if we hired somebody who really likes repairing cars, subscribes to car magazines, and has grown up in an environment where his father, or maybe an older brother, was always tinkering with an automobile or two.

It is also important for us to test, even after people have been hired. But once they're on board, the ultimate test should be applied by the customer, not a clinical psychologist. After all, you no longer have to create theoretical situations to see how they'll do on the job. They're *on* the job, and the customers (both internal and external) can tell you exactly how well they're doing.

Our Customer Satisfaction Index (CSI) is a form of on-the-job testing.

When General Motors created the industry's first CSI, some dealers —especially those who ended up with low CSI scores—thought GM's methodology was all wrong.

We didn't know who to believe, GM or the unhappy dealers, so we hired a firm to assist us in finding out who was right. They helped us

MANAGEMENT PROFILE

FACTOR A: MANAGEMENT APPROACH		5%		20%		50%		20%			5%
		9	(High)	8	7	6	5	4	3	2	(Low)	1
1)	Intensity	9	(High)	●	7	6	5	4	3	2	(Low)	1
2)	Control	9	(High)	8	7	6	●	4	3	2	(Low)	1
3)	Toughness											
a)	Mental	●	(High)	8	7	6	5	4	3	2	(Low)	1
b)	Emotional	9	(High)	●	7	6	5	4	3	2	(Low)	1
c)	Endurance	9	(High)	●	7	6	5	4	3	2	(Low)	1
4)	Plan and Analyze	9	(High)	8	7	6	5	●	3	2	(Low)	1
5)	Orientation											
a)	Sales	9	(High)	8	7	●	5	4	3	2	(Low)	1
b)	Administration	9	(High)	8	7	6	5	4	●	2	(Low)	1
c)	People	9	(High)	8	7	●	5	4	3	2	(Low)	1

FACTOR B: PERSONAL TENDENCIES

		9		8	7	6	5	4	3	2		1
6)	Intelligence	●	(High)	8	7	6	5	4	3	2	(Low)	1
7)	Status Needs	9	(High)	8	7	6	5	4	●	2	(Low)	1
8)	Recognition Needs	9	(High)	8	7	6	●	4	3	2	(Low)	1
9)	Self-direction	9	(High)	8	●	6	5	4	3	2	(Low)	1
10)	Routine Details	9	(High)	8	7	6	●	4	3	2	(Low)	1

FACTOR C: COMPANY FIT

		9		8	7	6	5	4	3	2		1
11)	Manageability	9	(High)	8	7	●	5	4	3	2	(Low)	1
12)	Policy-minded	9	(High)	●	7	6	5	4	3	2	(Low)	1

SUMMARY

		9		8	7	6	5	4	3	2		1
13)	Endorsement	9	(High)	8	●	6	5	4	3	2	(Low)	1
14)	Developmental Potential	9	(High)	8	●	6	5	4	3	2	(Low)	1

Primary Assets	Primary Liabilities
-- Intelligence	
-- Mental Toughness	
-- Positive Attitude	
-- Self-reliant	

Name _____   Results To _____

Position ___Parts & Service Director___   Date ___August 21, 1989___

REMARKS ___Above-average candidate for proposed position and potential to grow. More people___ oriented than typical candidate for service position. Self-starter, self-reliant, and highly durable. Should learn quickly and show above-average problem-solving capabilities. Overall performance should be consistently effective.

administer an extensive survey to see how customers felt about our people and the service they were providing.

If you had asked me who our best service advisers were, before we asked our customers, I would have named Rich Parker and another guy who had been with us a long time. And if you had asked me who were the worst, I would have said, "well, I'm not so sure about Clarence Diggs. And that Dan Weiss? He's from up North and talks funny [i.e., he didn't have a drawl], and I'm not so sure he has it down yet."

But when the results came in our top three were Clarence Diggs, Dan Weiss, and Rich Parker. The other guy didn't score so well. He had been around a long time, we all liked him, and he's the most technically knowledgeable of any of our service advisers, but his customers thought he wasn't paying as much attention to them as he should. (We shared the survey results with him and now he's doing a great job.)

The only thing wrong with Diggs and Weiss was that I didn't know them. Since I didn't know them, I doubted their ability.

I think that's very human. When I was in Rome, trying to help my sister after she had been in a car accident, I thought the doctors I met who spoke English were much brighter than the doctors who didn't. How illogical. But that was my gut reaction. I could understand them, so I liked them better.

I didn't know Dan Weiss and Clarence Diggs as well as I did the other guys, so I liked them less. But now I have their survey results and know how their customers feel about them, and that has nailed it for me. We're going to have continuous testing from now on.

Testing isn't a perfect screening device. It's an inexact science, but it's one that's made our hiring process a little bit better. The odds of somebody working out were about one in four before we started testing, and now they're better than one in two. That makes testing a hell of a good deal.

But, important as the test is, it only makes up about a third of our assessment about an applicant. The interviews count a lot more. Because they do, we have more than one person interview everyone who applies for a job. After the manager has talked to the applicant, we have him spend some time with another two or three employees so they can see what he's like.

The very last thing we do is have a couple of our people take the person to breakfast or lunch. That gives us a chance to evaluate him in a social setting.

The primary purpose of taking him out for a meal is to discover whether we like being around him. If we don't want to spend time with him, the customer probably won't either.

CHECKLIST

✔ *Smart is good.* Test for intelligence. All other things being equal, it's better to hire someone who's bright than someone who isn't.

✔ *Test to a template.* Test the best performers and try to hire more people like them.

✔ *Interview as many people as you can* . . . for each available job. You'll probably have to talk to twenty-five different people before you're really sure you've found the best person.

✔ *Ask about their past successes.* People who have performed well in the past will probably perform well in the future.

✔ *Are they going to fit in?* The best person in the world is going to have a hard time if he doesn't fit in. If your employees tend to be as subtle as a sledgehammer with each other, you might want to think twice before you hire someone who is very sensitive.

CHAPTER 17

Developing service superstars

After we hire people they attend a new employee orientation meeting—where we talk about our history and how we expect our people to treat customers—and we assign everyone a "training partner," someone who's doing the same job they are and from whom they can learn company policy, or maybe just where the restroom is. When you're in a strange new situation, there's nothing better than having a friend, someone who can explain to you the folklore, culture, and rituals.

We also try to communicate to our new employees who our heroes are, people who exemplify success around here. In sales, we talk about Jerry Griffin, now general manager at Sewell Village Cadillac, who when he was a salesman sold more cars (retail) than any other Cadillac salesman in the country. In his best year he sold 712, and years when he sold 500 were pretty common.

Jerry was an all-Southwest Conference linebacker at SMU and used the same hardworking, aggressive approach he brought to football to sell cars. He came to work at seven-thirty, and he didn't go home until the last customer left, usually after 9 P.M. He never left for lunch. He always brought it in a brown paper bag and ate at his desk. He didn't take a vacation for five years.

Jerry first began to work for us during the off season, while he was still playing pro football. (He was an all-pro linebacker for the Edmonton Eskimos in the CFL.) As a college graduate, he was embarrassed to be selling cars. In fact, it made him so uncomfortable, he didn't tell his mother for two years. When he finally let her know what he did for a living, he gave her a new Cadillac to cushion the blow. Since then they've both decided the car business is great.

Jerry was successful because of the way he went about selling cars. There wasn't anything he wouldn't do for a customer. One day the Dr. Pepper Company sent out bid sheets to all the Cadillac dealers in the area, asking for prices on what would become the chairman's car. Instead of merely filling out the form, Jerry had four Cadillacs driven to the company parking lot and asked the chairman, W. W. Clements, to "come outside and pick out your new car." Clements, who has since retired, admired Jerry's salesmanship, and the service, and bought the car on the spot. He has remained a customer ever since.

Another hero is Rich Parker, who sold more parts and service work in one year ($2 million) than any service adviser we've ever heard of. But, more important, he also received more complimentary letters from our customers than all our seven other service advisers combined. Rich has more true empathy for customers than anyone I have ever seen. It's not unusual for him to meet with customers at the service department after hours, or on Sunday, and he'd even make house calls, if that was what needed to be done to take care of one of his customers. Rich is now service manager at Sewell Village Cadillac.

Neither of these men went entirely by the book, and sometimes that was disruptive. (Stealing three people out of the service department to take those cars over to Dr. Pepper was not well received by the service manager.) But, in the final analysis, they made the sale and/or made the customer happy. That's what matters. That's why we consider Griffin and Parker (and all the other people we don't have space to mention) "heroes," even if they didn't always do things exactly by the rules.

We try to encourage mavericks, people with a little rebellion in their souls. Those kinds of people seem to do well. Our very best managers, salespeople, and technicians rarely do everything exactly by the numbers, but they get the job done better than someone who dots every *i*, because they're creative and determined. That's why we talk about our heroes to new employees.

Although it's important to talk about heroes, and what new employees should do, it's equally important that people know what *not* to do. People who leave on time, take all their days off, and can't take a joke don't do well here.

Integrity is a big deal, only outstanding performers get promoted, and if you mistreat a customer, you'll lose your job.

What we tell people is that when we review them, which happens automatically after they have been here sixty days, they'll be judged on three criteria:

✱ Are they a fit? *We want to know what both their colleagues and their customers think of them.*

✱ Can they do the job? *It doesn't matter if everyone likes them if they don't do enough work and do it correctly.*

∗ Are they showing significant improvement? *Not only do we want to know that they are getting better at what they do, we're looking for signs that they're capable of taking on more responsibility.*

If the answers to these three questions are no—and there are no extenuating circumstances—we'll consider trying the employee at something else. The management books seem to say that, if you're willing to spend the time, you can teach anybody how to do a good job. I won't say the books are wrong, but in a small company like ours it's just easier to replace a person who's having an awful lot of problems. We don't have the resources to spend a lot of time with someone if he's nonproductive and doesn't care about customers. We can't afford to wait until someone "finds" himself. The competition is too fierce for that. It isn't a sin to fire someone.

That's especially true if someone holds a pivotal position, a job that will determine whether or not the firm will be successful. These are what Steve Mulvany, president of Management Tools—an Orange, California, company that is the recognized expert in creating and implementing effective performance systems—calls "gamebreaker positions."

In baseball, you can't win without great pitching.

In football, you need a great quarterback.

In basketball, you need a great playmaker.

It's no different in business. The gamebreaker positions—for example, loan officers at a bank; pilots at the airlines; and the editor responsible for acquiring and publishing this book (Hi, Harriet)—cannot be left in the hands of average people.

Our gamebreakers are our department managers, the people in charge of new cars, used cars, service, finance and insurance, parts, body shop, and our controller. These people determine our success or failure because they—much more than I—affect our relationship with our customers and determine how profitable we will be.

If the person in any one of these positions is performing at an average level or below, we immediately try to find out why. Has he received adequate training? Does he have the necessary experience? Does he really have the ability to do the job?

If the answer to all these questions is yes, and the job still is not getting done, you have to make a move. Don't let someone remain in a gamebreaker position if he's not performing. In a position that's this important, average is absolutely unacceptable, no matter how much you like the employee, how long he's been with you, or how good a job he used to do. Move him—you don't have to fire him—somewhere else.

You can sit around endlessly discussing all the mitigating circumstances that are keeping someone in a gamebreaker position from getting the job done. But quit talking and go with your gut instinct and make a move—and do it sooner rather than later.

CHECKLIST

✔ *Once you've hired someone* . . . talk about what it takes to succeed in your company. Give examples of your company's values and its "heroes."

✔ *Don't be afraid to fire folks.* Work real hard with marginal performers, but once it becomes clear that somebody is not going to work out, let him go. It's best for the employee and the company.

✔ *Hire mavericks.* The best performers always know how to bend the rules to get the job done for the customer—and the company.

FOUR

How do you know how good you are?

CHAPTER 18

Accounting for more than money

Think about what happened the last time you went out to play tennis. How long did it take, after you had been rallying for a while, for someone to say, "Want to play a set?"

What they were really saying was, "Let's keep score." We all, whether we're out on the court or on the job, like to know how well we're doing. And the only way of finding out is by keeping score.

Counting the number of things we sell is one way of keeping score. It gives us an overall picture.

That's good, but it's not enough. It's not, for example, anywhere close to what's done in baseball. While you are watching a ball game on television, you'll see flashed up on the screen how this batter does against left-handed pitchers at night, playing on Astroturf. Everyone knows how he hits with men on base and whether he has a higher batting average during the first part of the game or in the later innings.

At work, we are nowhere near as sophisticated. But we should be. We should know exactly how we're doing, so we can find out where we should improve. The only way we are going to find that out is by measuring everything that we possibly can. And we do.

Some people think that's wrong. They don't measure much of anything. They just tell people, "Do the best you can."

That's silly.

It's silly because doing the best you can may not be good enough. It's just like sports. Say we are talking about running the 100 meters. If the very best a runner can do is 15 seconds, then sorry, folks, it just ain't good enough. He's just not going to win, no matter who he knows or how smart he is.

We all compete in some kind of marketplace—be it the Olympics or business—and doing our best is not what's required. We've got to be better than the competition. We've got to be the best.

That's why we measure performance—of everybody including me. (My report card is the company's P & L.) We want to know how everyone's doing and, equally important, we want to know what it's going to take to be the best. If the record for the 100 meters is 9.9, and someone's running 15 flat, then we know his time must be cut by at least 5.1 seconds.

Management consultant Steve Mulvany has been instrumental in improving our productivity. He's helped me understand the importance of measurements, feedback, and recognition.

Steve came to understand the relationship between measurements and performance when he was still in school. Let him tell you about it.

> When I was in college, I worked in a cannery each summer during the tomato crop season. My job was twofold: first, to turn off the machine, if something went wrong. That was easier said than done, since the machine ran at a rate of 650 cans per minute. If I didn't *hear* the problem, the machine would suddenly jam, causing 190 degree tomato juice to squirt right at my belly.
>
> The second part of my job was to put lids into the canning machine— real boring. In fact, I knew if I didn't make my job more interesting, I was going to go nuts—the fellow next to me was nuts.
>
> I began to keep score of my performance. The company counted the number of cases, total fluid ounces, operating minutes, downtime, and maintenance costs on my machine.
>
> I counted lids.
>
> I could see and touch lids. In fact, every day I kept track of how many cases of lids I completed, multiplied cases by 3,600 (the number of lids per case) to reach the total lids run that day through my machine. Daily, I would write my score on a lunch bag.
>
> After four days of keeping score, I found myself trying to beat my best day, and figuring out how many lids I would have to load an hour to achieve a record pace.
>
> The company didn't know I was counting, still my machine achieved the highest production of any in the plant.
>
> Everybody counts. Whether the person is making sales calls, typing letters, repairing automobiles, mining coal, or canning tomato juice, he is keeping track of a score. Management's challenge is to create a measurement and feedback system which is interesting and relevant for the individual or the team.

We liked Mulvany's ideas, so we asked him to help us set up a measurement system that made sense.

He started by giving us a choice of things we could measure.

I. *Quantity*

   A Dollar amount of sales

   B Number of units completed

   C Orders shipped

   D Calls completed

II. *Quality*

   A Number of items completed correctly

   B Percent of retained customers

   C Ratio of positive to negative letters

   D Service feedback scores (customer satisfaction index)

   E Employee retention/turnover

III. *Cost*

   A Total cost per unit sold

   B Labor cost

   C Budget vs. actual

   D Accounts receivable

   E Costs per square foot

IV. *Timeliness*

   A Average turnaround time to process orders

   B Percentage of on-time delivery

   C Percent of items completed within 48 hours

Having figured out the kinds of things we wanted to measure—we'll talk about them in a minute—Mulvany gave us four questions to think about before we put the performance measurements in place. Again, we'll let Mulvany explain:

IS THE MEASUREMENT IMPORTANT?

Will the employees relate to the indicator? Are the data available at least every two weeks? (Data posted less often are not effective for performance feedback.) If you stopped tracking the data, would anybody care? If improved, will this measure have a significant impact on the company or department?

IS THE MEASUREMENT EASY TO TRACK?

If the score takes anyone more than 15 minutes per day to track, it's probably not feasible to do it. The easiest way to set up a tracking system is to look at the data you are already collecting. Think about how you might set up automated collection systems on your micro, mini, or mainframe computers.

WILL THE EMPLOYEES UNDERSTAND THE MEASUREMENT?

There are some management measures (return on investment, inventory turns, days receivable outstanding, etc.) which would not be commonly understood by nonmanagement staff. The most effective measures are simply stated. Putting things in terms of units is best, dollars are second best, third best would be percentages. Ironically, management usually relates to things in exactly the reverse order—percentages, then dollars and, finally, units.)

IS THE MEASUREMENT STATED IN POSITIVE TERMS?

If you can measure absenteeism, you can track attendance. Instead of scrap, report yield. Don't measure late deliveries, track on-time shipments.

People would much rather shoot for a goal than avoid making a mistake.

More important, if you only report what's undesirable, people may not be sure what they are supposed to accomplish.

After Mulvany had explained all of this to us, we sat down and tried to figure out how we should create our measurement goals. It turned out to be a five-step process.

First, we had to determine what was the right thing to measure. For a salesperson it would be the number of cars he sold in a month. For a receivables clerk, it might be the average number of days it takes her to collect a bill.

Second, having figured out what to measure, we needed to find out what the industry average was. Everybody has a trade association, and most of them track those kinds of numbers.

The average becomes the minimum score we will find acceptable. Our goal always is to end up in the top 5%. Our salesmen are a good example of how this works.

Back in 1957 when we began tracking the number of cars each salesperson sold, our people were selling 6 cars a month, and that was about the national average. So we set our first goal at 8 cars a month. Once we reached 8, we raised it to 10, and we've steadily increased it ever since. Today, nobody feels like they've had a great month unless they've sold 20 or more. We expect them to sell 15.

Over the last thirty-three years the nationwide average has also increased—to 8.

Why do we keep raising our expectations?

So we don't get complacent. It's easy to get sloppy once you've achieved your goal. To ensure that that doesn't happen, you always need to find a bigger mountain to climb. You have to keep continually raising your standards—both to keep your people sharp and to stay ahead of the competition. Once you're satisfied, you can be sure that someone is going to pass you right by. You can never, never stop raising your standard of performance.

It's a funny thing about goals. Initially, when you announce them, a lot of people say they're impossible; there's no way that anyone will ever be able to reach them. But it's like what happened with the four-minute mile. For the longest time, people said no one would ever be able to run that fast. But once Roger Bannister did, the times just kept getting faster and faster to the point where the record is now 3:46 (Steve Cram).

The same thing happened in the high jump. Everybody said no one would be able to jump 8 feet. But then Javier Sotomayor, a Cuban, did it in 1989, and all of a sudden we had a whole bunch of people jumping 7 feet 11 inches. It won't be long before they'll be over 8 feet too, but somebody had to break that barrier first.

It's no different with selling cars. In 1989, when we first set the goal of selling 20 Hyundais a month, everyone said it couldn't be done. And it *is* hard, because for every sale you actually make you probably have to close two or three. Many Hyundai buyers have a hard time qualifying for financing. Usually the Hyundai is their first new car and they don't have much of a credit history. So 20 cars a month is a challenge, one that many of our Hyundai salesmen thought would never be met.

But then Mel Warren, one of the most professionally competitive human beings I have ever met, came along and sold 20 Hyundais in a month—in fact, he sold 26. So now a bunch of our other salespeople are saying, "If he can sell 20, I can sell 20. [Three did it recently.] But what I'm really going to do is break Warren's record."

People are naturally competitive. They'll try to exceed whatever goals are set for them, whether or not they're paid more for doing so. Since that's true, the secret is to set goals that are in the best interest of the business.

And that's an interesting thing about setting goals. People will play to them—even if they don't get paid anything extra for meeting them. (Chapter 20 explains how we pay folks.) People are naturally competitive; they'll try to exceed whatever expectations are set for them.

When we started quantifying everything, the guys who deliver the cars to our customers once the repairs are finished came to us and asked to see the results of the customer survey questions that pertained to them. When we gave them the totals, one of the things they picked up on was the question which asked, "How long did you have to wait for your car, once you had paid your bill?"

We had been tracking the time—it was somewhere around six minutes—but they never knew how they were doing. Once we showed them their times, they all had the same question: "Who's the fastest?" Ever since then, we've posted their times. They've all started running, and the average is down to about three minutes. They take great pride in doing it under three minutes—that's the goal they've set for themselves—and if they find a technician parked the car in the wrong place, and they have to go searching for it (which, of course, increases their time), they're likely to go back to his stall and raise a little hell.

This is strictly a competitive thing. They don't get a bonus if they bring the car up in less than three minutes. They just like to brag a little about their times and kid the folks who are a bit slower. That's why our customers are now getting their cars more quickly than ever before.

All this is really pretty logical. Think of the last time you played racquetball with a friend. Odds are, you were running all over the court and banging into walls, trying to make a shot, and you weren't getting paid anything. You just wanted to win.

This is just human nature. People like to compete whether they are six or sixty.

We hired a salesman who was in his sixties and was used to selling eight or nine cars a month at the dealership he had been with for a long time. When he came here he discovered, of course, our expectations are a lot higher.

He looked around at all our guys, who routinely outsold him by an average of two to one, and said, "I don't want to retire and twiddle my thumbs. I can compete with these young whippersnappers!" And he really got going. He's now selling 50% more cars than he used to, all because he wasn't going to let somebody else show him up.

We're all made like that.

Since we are, we measure everything and post the results so everyone has a chance to compete. The times of the people delivering cars can be found near the service area; in the receivables department there are charts like the one on page 89, and the dealership's CSI is posted all over. (Not everything is on display. While we track a salesperson's gross profit per car, that kind of information is put into a book that is available to all our salespeople but not to our customers.)

The charts and graphs we do post are personalized. Every technician, for example, has a plaque over his work area that shows his name, and on it are spaces to place the small (2 inches in diameter) Cadillac wreath and crest sticker we award to everyone who did 100% of his work correctly for a month.

In addition, every technician's performance is charted and posted, so that at a glance he can know exactly how his 96% quality rating—the number produced by dividing the number of jobs he did right by his total number of jobs that month—compares to the score of every other technician. (It would make him about average.) The more you post, the more effective it is. And because we believe Mulvany is right, we track the number of jobs done correctly. It would be demeaning to display the number of mistakes publicly.

We post the results and personalize them so that everybody understands how the game is played and who's doing the best. The chart doesn't track how long it takes the receivables department to collect a bill. It's labeled "Beth's Accounts Receivable." And in departments like receivables, where

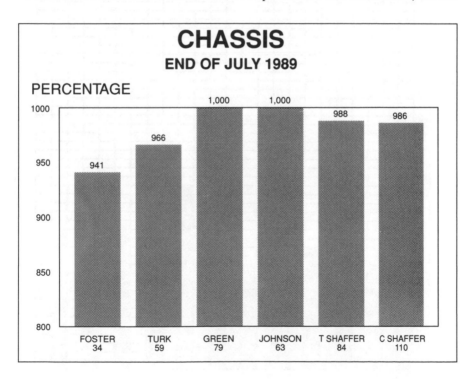

there is only one person working, we chart her performance over a twelve-month period, so that she's able to see long-term trends, in addition to doing a month-to-month comparison.

At first, not all our employees like the idea of having their scores posted, especially if they aren't doing a good job. But nobody is going to

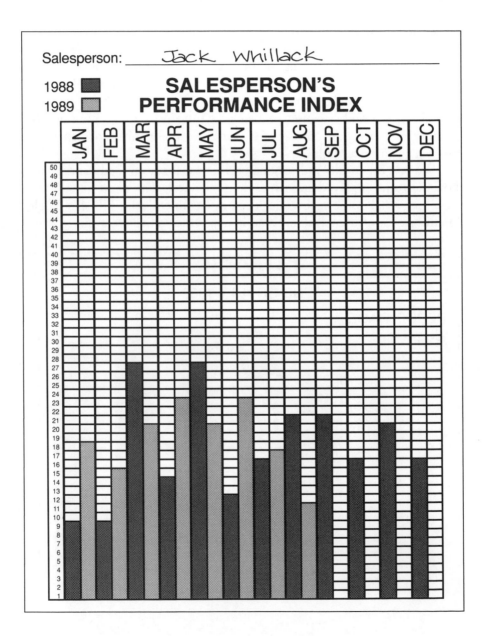

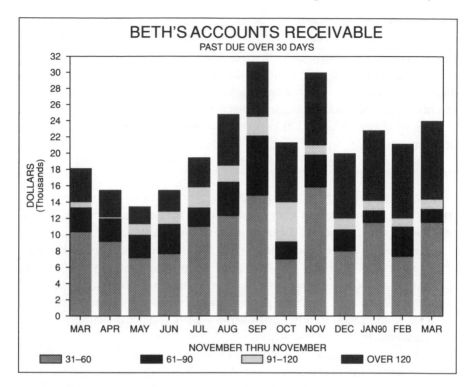

die over this. And if they are consistently doing a bad job, they're not going to be here for long. No one wants them around.

There's another reason why people accept the charts and graphs: we only measure things that affect their job.

It's not as if we take all the service technicians out back, have them run the 40-yard dash, and then post their times. We only chart their job performance, something that's within their control. They may not be able to help the fact that they don't run very fast, but they sure as heck can ensure they did that last tune-up correctly. Those are the kinds of things we measure.

If we are going to make this big a deal about measuring performance, then we have to make sure that what we measure is fair and factual.

Let's take fair first.

Suppose we're measuring the work done by two technicians, and one guy has an easy job, like washing cars, and the other one is repairing transmissions. Some people might think the transmission work is more important than the car wash. But the customer doesn't. The customer wants *everything* done right.

So both jobs are equally important. Each person would receive the gold wreath and crest, and public recognition, for doing his or her work correctly. We do, however, pay them differently. Obviously, the technician who works on transmissions will make more.

As for being factual, count the things that are important and count them right, and give the person whose work you're measuring a chance to point out when you've made a mistake.

We're always asked: "Do people get bonuses for turning in superior performances?"

There are two answers: "Not necessarily," and "Usually not."

That is not un-American.

First, remember how we pay people. Since they're paid for each job completed, the more work they do, the more money they'll make. Those additional payments aren't a bonus; they've earned it.

The second answer about not paying bonuses relates again to the type of people who work here. We hire good people, and we pay them more than the competition does, because they consistently turn in a superior performance. In fact, superior performances have become standard.

The woman who handles our warranty work is a great example of how this all works.

When you buy a car, the manufacturer promises that some things won't go wrong for a certain amount of time. The battery will keep working for at least three years, for example. Or certain things are included for free. Lexus, for example, doesn't charge people for their first two regularly scheduled service visits.

But even though that work is free to customers, dealers still get paid for doing it. After we've completed the warranty work, the manufacturers reimburse us. It's one of their costs of doing business.

We have one person who's in charge of these warranty receivables. When she got the job, they were averaging 45 days. It took 45 days from the time we replaced the battery until General Motors sent us a check for the work.

That was just too long. In trying to figure out how long it should take, we asked—as we always do—"What is the norm?" And with warranty receivables, it turns out, 15 days is the national average. So did she get a bonus for cutting it from 45 days to 15? No.

(She eventually reduced it to 9 days, and we gave her a small raise.)

But again, it's usually not the money that's the motivating force. People will walk by her desk and see the chart that shows warranty receivables are down to 9 days and say, "That's great!" Her manager will take her out to lunch, and in general people in her department will make a big deal out of what a great job she's done.

Some people listen to how we've set up our measurement systems and say: "It wouldn't work for me. I'm not motivated that way. I wouldn't work any harder just because my performance was posted."

Bull. People know how much work they've done, and they're either proud of the amount they do or embarrassed by it. Besides, people really like to know how they're doing.

Now some jobs are harder to measure than others—which gets back to the importance of measuring fairly—but you can always come up with something relevant to measure: the number of cars sold, or items processed, or hamburgers cooked on your shift.

Mulvany and Deming say we take measurement as a form of motivation to an extreme. Normally, they like businesses to measure the production of a team or a department. How many french fries were sold by the evening shift at McDonald's, and that sort of thing.

I think that's fine, but I also want to track how each individual did. Again, it's like baseball. It's great to know whether your team won or lost, but you also want to know who went zero for four, or four for four.

Is there a danger that people will just concentrate on their own stats, at the expense of the team? Sure, but that danger exists in sports too. That's why we have coaches (and bosses).

CHECKLIST

✔ *Measure what's relevant.* You cannot tell people to do their best and then hope their best is good enough. You (and they) have to know how they're doing and where they—and the business—can improve.

✔ *Post results.* Be fair and factual in your measurements, but once you know how everyone is doing, post the results and share the information. People are naturally competitive, want to do a good job, and like to know how they're doing.

✔ *Keep raising the level of acceptable performance.* Once your goals have been achieved, you have to keep raising your sights. Unless you're consistently getting better, somebody will pass you by.

✔ *Limit your goals.* If you give people too many things to concentrate on, they won't be able to concentrate on anything. Set no more than five goals—one may be all you need.

FIVE

What do you pay to get good service?

CHAPTER 19

Save more by paying more

If we're going to attract superior people—whether they're technicians or controllers—we need to pay them more.

We should *want* to pay our people more than they could make elsewhere. We want people to have pride in their work. A bigger paycheck helps. No, the amount of money employees get paid is not the most important thing in determining how they feel about their jobs—in fact, most people put it fifth or sixth on the list—but it is a factor, and one I don't want to dismiss lightly. I don't think anyone in our organization will say they're underworked. And in our surveys, not too many of them say that they are overpaid. They feel they earn their money, and they do in the way they take care of our customers and how hard they work.

One of the questions we constantly ask our people is: "How can we help you make more money?"

Are we wasting money by "overpaying"?

I don't think so.

Good people make fewer mistakes. So we get greater efficiency.

More important, they tend to be more productive and resourceful.

We try to hire only smart people who understand how we do things. Those kinds of people will be more productive and go out of their way to provide excellent customer service, without having someone hovering over their shoulders all the time. So, not only will they do a better job than the kinds of employees our competition hires, but we'll need fewer people to supervise them. That lowers our costs.

In fact, I know that paying our people more makes us more efficient. It sounds strange but it's true. Take our salespeople for example.

Let's say an automobile dealership sells 100 cars a month. As you've seen, the typical salesperson sells 8 cars a month. That means the dealership has about twelve salespeople.

But we can sell 100 cars a month with only eight salespeople. That means we need four less desks on the sales floor—after all, I don't have twelve guys on the floor, just eight. That means we need four fewer phone lines, and there are four fewer people on the payroll.

So we save a lot of money, plus we can attract better salespeople, because our people make more here than they could working for somebody else. Our average Chevrolet salesperson is selling about 12.5 cars a month (100 cars divided by our eight salespeople) while a salesperson working for our competition is only averaging 8. (Their 100 cars, remember, are being sold by twelve people.)

Where would you rather work? At a place where salespeople average 8 cars a month, or one where you could sell 50% more? The fact that you can make a lot more money at our place becomes known within the industry, and the better salespeople apply for jobs. We're creating an upward spiral of quality, thanks to how we pay, yet our costs per car sold falls because we need fewer salespeople. Everyone wins.

The same thing holds true for our technicians. Let's say at the average dealership a technician can do six tune-ups during an eight-hour shift. Well, during the same eight hours our guys can do eight. Why? Because we don't waste their time. They don't have to go searching for the next car to work on. We have a computerized system that tracks where each car is. And they don't have to stand around waiting for the parts they need. In fact, if it's a part they use at least once a week, it will be stored in a cabinet at their workbench. We make sure they have the right equipment. And they're well trained, so they don't have to spend a lot of time figuring out how a repair should be done. They'll know before they go to work.

We pay our technicians exactly what other dealers do for doing a tune-up—and we charge our customers the same rate, too—but our technicians get to make 33% more money (and so do we) because they're a third more productive during the day.

Now, one of the things that can happen under our system is that people can make an awful lot of money. That's just fine by us, but it makes some employers nervous. They worry that they're paying people "too" much.

That doesn't make me nervous. It's great. In fact, one of the questions my managers and I are constantly asking is: How can we help you make more money? In other words, what can we do to make you more productive? When we asked the technicians that question, they came up with the ideas that led to our developing the computerized tracking system which makes it easier for them to find the next car to work on. We implemented their suggestions and now they have more time to spend doing their job. They make more money, and so do we.

This just strikes us as common sense, but many businesses go out of their way to do just the opposite.

Often, if somebody is doing real well in a sales territory, a company will divide it up, because they think the salesperson is making too much. That's wrong. Why not help him make even more? Get him an assistant. If he's really doing well, and his market share is right and his margins are good, let him make a lot of money. Why cut his pay? Why destroy his incentive? That's un-American. Let him make as much as he can. If you've got a true superstar, let him run. When he makes more money, so will the company.

Here's my favorite example of that. Curley Crawford was the man who really turned our service, parts, and body shop departments around and made them outstanding. Crawford is a true hero in our organization. When we promoted him from transmission technician to service director, his compensation was $27,500 a year plus 10% of any increase in profits in his departments. The service department was unprofitable at the time.

By the end of the second year he was making $75,000. When he got his W-2, he told a couple of his friends here, "They're never gonna let me make this much money. They're going to cut my pay. You watch, they're going to change the arrangement."

I thought that was kind of funny. We hadn't considered changing his pay, and we didn't change it.

The next year he made $100,000, and he said: "Well, they're gonna cut it this year for sure."

So I called him in for a review and I said, "Curley, we need to talk about your pay."

And all his body language said, "I knew it! He's gonna be like everybody else. He's going to cut my pay." He just sat there and stared at me.

I said, "I'm really proud of the job you've done and hope you make a lot more money next year."

Two years later he was making $150,000, and I called him back in and I knew he was waiting for me to change his deal. He had the same expression on his face, the same body language.

And I said, "You did a great job, and we are going to keep everything exactly as it is."

He said, "You aren't ever gonna change my pay plan, are you?"

I said no. There was no reason to. Sure, his 10% share of the increase in profits was adding up to be a lot of money, but the dealership was getting the other 90%. Why would we want to take away the incentive of a man who had done such a great job?

It's management's job to design a system that allows the worker to perform at his highest level, and when he reaches it he should be able to make more. That's only fair, since he'll be making more money for the company.

CHECKLIST

✔ *Pay more, willingly.* You've gone out of your way to hire the best people. Pay them a premium over what they could get by working for the competition.

✔ *That extra money is not a gift.* People should know they're going to earn that premium by being more productive and providing their customers with "extras."

✔ *You'll get a good return on this investment.* That extra money you're paying won't be wasted. It will allow you to hire more talented people who'll work more efficiently. Good people make fewer mistakes, need less supervision, and are more willing to do whatever needs to be done to make the customer happy.

✔ *Don't change the rules in the middle of the game.* If it turns out that people are making a lot of money, don't cut their pay. Figure out ways they—and the company—can make even more.

CHAPTER 20

Partnership pay

It may sound funny, but if you really want your people to provide the best service they possibly can, eliminate their salaries. Pay them like a partner.

Partnership pay can take many forms. It can be as simple as putting *everyone* on commission, or paying people for each job they do. You can even give employees a percentage of the net profits. But no matter what form it takes, partnership pay is a very adult approach to compensation. It lets the people creating the company's income share in that income. It also clarifies for everyone exactly where the money comes from.

Since employees are now sharing in the company's profits, they have a vested interest in cutting costs, increasing sales, and improving quality.

Some jobs (sales) are best compensated on the basis of individual performance. Other jobs (manufacturing; accounting) should be evaluated by how well the department or team does. But once a fair and accurate measurement system is developed, the concept of partnership pay is a pretty darn fair system.

This approach to compensation works at all levels of the business, so we employ it company-wide. Executives are paid a percentage of the net produced by the department they're responsible for.

Where there are potential conflicts, people are paid out of the same pool. We need to make sure that the interests of our employees and of our dealership are the same when it comes to how people get paid. We call this concept parallel pay.

In our company, we sell new and used cars. And if you paid the new car manager solely out of the profit of the new car department, and the used car manager solely from the profit of the used car department, there'd be a heck of a fight when it came to valuing trade-ins. After all, the new car salesman wants the trade-in to be as high as possible, to help him make the deal. But the used car manager wants it to be as low as possible so that he can have the greatest profit when it comes time to resell the car.

So what we do is combine the departments' profit and loss statements and pay the managers out of the combined profit. That way, they both win and lose together, and have a common goal. Equally important, their interests and the company's are now identical.

The same concept applies to technicians. If they do more tune-ups, they should be paid more, provided that we are making a profit on that work and the work is done right. If the customer has to bring the car back because the technician did the work incorrectly, nobody gets paid for rework. Not the technician and not the company. We both lose, which is another example of parallel pay.

Once we have the pay plans parallel, the partnership pay system works just fine—it has for the last twenty years. Periodically, though, we test it, just to make sure. I remember we had an excellent technician who was working in the make ready department—that's where we put on the hub-caps, fix anything on the car that might not be exactly right when it's delivered from the factory, and add accessories like compact disc players —and we were paying him by the piece. We kept track of his work and, as an experiment, we took him off commission and put him on salary, paying him what he had averaged for the six months before. His production went to one half what it had been. Quality didn't change. He did quality work before, he did quality after, but his productivity went down. He was no longer a partner.

I think a lot of times low productivity comes about because nobody is keeping score. Nobody is counting the number of jobs a person is doing right. Nobody knows how long a job should take. If you kept real good score, you could get almost as much productivity out of a person as you could if you paid him like a partner, because people are naturally com-petitive. If I know you're doing ten oil changes a day, and that's more than anybody else, I am going to try real hard to do eleven.

But partnership pay is even better. People see an absolute correlation between the work they do and the money they earn, if they are given a percentage of the profits or are paid by the piece.

If they're real hungry, they can work late and make enough money for the payment on a boat, or they can come in early and get some extra work in so they'll have a little extra for Christmas. On the sales floor, they can work longer during the day, or work more nights or Saturdays, to sell more cars. People will find a range of work where they feel comfortable, and hopefully that will be within the range the company finds acceptable.

Partnership pay encourages employees to serve customers well. It's in their self-interest to do the job right and be nice, because they know it's the customer who determines how much they'll be paid.

(That's one of the things you work out as a manager. You have to create incentives for the high-end producers—you want to keep them motivated—and incentives and discipline for the low-end producers.) If someone is happy selling 6 cars a month, he might need to work for someone else.

Now there's an obvious question to ask about all this: doesn't partnership pay, which appeals so strongly to someone's self-interest, undercut our attempt to provide excellent customer service? Won't people be in such a hurry to get the work done, in order to earn their part of the profits, that they'll short-change the customer?

The answer is no. They'll continue to be warm, friendly, and efficient *to keep the customer coming back.* It's in their self-interest to do that because, if the customer comes back and buys something else, they'll make more money and the company will prosper. They'll earn a second commission on that second sale. And since it's far easier to sell a product to someone you already have a relationship with than it is to sell a stranger, people are going to be sure to treat their customers well.

It becomes a self-fulfilling prophecy. If you treat the customer well, he likes you. If he likes you, he'll buy more. If he buys more, you make more money, so you keep treating him well.

And there's an added benefit. If you treat your customers well, they'll tell their friends, who then come in, and you make even more money.

Okay, you say, but if the salesman is running all over the place trying to help a current customer with whatever he needs, he's not going to be on the sales floor greeting new ones. That means at the end of the week his check is going to be smaller than it might have been if he had been less accommodating.

That's not true. At the end of the month his total will be greater than the one turned in by a salesman who isn't as customer driven. Over time, his satisfied customers will keep coming back, and so will their friends. We know that's true, because we've documented it. What we've found is that the salespeople with the highest CSI, the ones who take the best care of their customers, make the most money. The dealers with the highest CSI are the most profitable and, equally important, they're the ones who remain in business during the hard times.

People—or places—that treat their customers badly just don't make it long term.

This way of paying people works.

Sometimes it's hard to get people to come to work in a place where they don't get a salary. It makes some people uncomfortable. If it does, we put that person on a declining salary base for a relatively short period of time—say ninety days. Here's how it works. The first month we'll pay him $3,000 in salary, plus whatever commission he earns. The second month, $2,000 plus commissions. In month three, $1,000 plus commissions. Starting the fourth month, he, like everyone else, is on straight commission. If after ninety days the employee doesn't feel comfortable with the way we pay people, he should be working someplace else, and that happens sometimes.

A guy who's an excellent technician can work on the assembly line at the GM-Arlington plant near us and do pretty well. He'll make about 30% less than he would under our system, but he'll think of it as regular. For people like that, the "regular paycheck" is a better deal.

It takes more of a self-reliant, self-starting person to function well under our kind of compensation system. It forces people to be more responsible for themselves. I think that's good for both our people and our company.

If you think about it, paying people based on commissions, piecework and/or a percentage of the net, is really profit sharing at its best. It not only creates a partnership, at the same time it lets people take responsibility for the work they do. It makes them feel more like independent contractors than employees.

It takes a little bit of work initially to set up a partnership pay plan. To make sure it is fair and effective, you have to figure out a logical way of quantifying the amount of work a person does. But doctors get paid this way, and so do lawyers. Hell, if they can figure it out, anybody can.

CHECKLIST

✔ *Pay for performance.* Put everybody on commission, piecework or a percentage of the net. It makes sense. People should only get paid for the work they do. Without excellent performance, there is no profit to share, and eventually no job or company.

✔ *Everybody means everybody.* Department managers, division heads, everyone should be paid like a partner, not just the owner.

✔ *This way of paying folks makes everyone want to take care of the customer.* Partnership pay actually improves customer service. If you want to be paid, you'll be nice to the people who are responsible for paying you—your customers.

SIX

Leadership is performance

CHAPTER 21

You can't fake it

I hate using the word "I" when talking about our business, because everything we do really is a team effort.

But in each organization a leader must step forward. He must make the company successful. He's got to provide jobs, ensure that the company turns a profit, and create a place where people are proud to work. If he doesn't do those things, no one will follow him. In the final analysis, the authority of a manager comes from the managed. As Peter Drucker says, "Leadership is performance."

If you're the boss, you can't fake it. You either believe in the goals you've set or you don't, and if you don't you're going to get found out. First, it takes too much effort to pretend. Second, employees watch their leaders too closely for them to be able to fake anything.

Once people catch you not caring about a goal you've set—you said we *always* have to treat customers honestly, and they watch while you deliberately short-change someone—it's all over. They'll stop caring because they see you don't.

Even when people know what they are supposed to do, sometimes they forget. That's why they hold church every Sunday.

It's also why you—through both word and deed—have to constantly remind people what your values are.

Once that happens, all the banners and pep rallies in the world aren't going to change things. You'll never achieve your goal.

107

Let me tell you a quick story about that. I was out of town during the day we opened our Lexus dealership, and we were mobbed from sunup to sundown. When I got back that night, I stopped by and saw that the carpenters—who were still working on the building as we opened—had left cups and empty boxes lying about outside.

I went around and started picking all that stuff up, and it wasn't very long before I had a couple of salesmen working next to me. I never had to ask them to help.

While we were cleaning up, one of the guys said, "You know, the contractor is supposed to do this."

And I said, "But they didn't, and this is our house, so we have to take care of it."

I think the message got across. But still, the people who work with you must hear you say this sort of thing over and over and over. They have to see you picking up the papers in the parking lot or carrying something out to the car for a customer. It's a way you establish and reinforce your company's values. That's why we write people up in the company newsletter when they've gone out of their way for a customer. It's also the reason we talk about our best employees as much as we do.

Repeating our values and beliefs over and over again is a lot like why they hold church every Sunday. You can't read the Bible just once and understand all of its lessons.

But even when you know what you're supposed to do you sometimes forget. That's why we go to church: to be reminded. And that's also why we keep repeating what we believe in—and celebrate each time we meet one of our goals: to remind ourselves.

Now, how many goals you should set is an interesting question. There are a lot of people who say one is enough. If you just have one goal, everybody can concentrate on it. Nobody will have to worry about anything else, and it will be easier to accomplish what you want done.

But, while that sounds good, it's not right. You could say our goal is to fix the job right the first time. But at the same time we want our employees to be polite and nice to customers. And we want our facility to be immaculate. On top of that, we expect you to treat your fellow workers well. Plus, we want to make a profit. Any of these five things could be *the goal*. But they're all important. Just concentrating on one wouldn't be enough.

However, if you keep adding on goals, you'll soon reach the point where you really are giving people too much to think about. At some point—probably around six or seven objectives—you'll be beyond the scope of the human mind. It's hard to keep more than half a dozen things straight.

But whether you set one goal or six, the only way you are going to accomplish any of them is by constantly talking about what you are trying to do (and why) and pointing out examples of where you're succeeding.

We're seeing a great example of that right now in Dallas. We're selling lots of cars when others aren't; and we're also doing a lot of service and parts and body work, while our competitors have lots of downtime.

I try to point this out over and over and over again. I don't do it by standing up in front of the troops; I prefer talking to people one on one. It's more effective to talk to a person directly; you know you have his attention. I'll spend some time with a salesman, technician, or manager and point out how they're making money, while many dealerships all over the country are in trouble or are going out of business.

Later, when they are having lunch with their colleagues, they'll get around to talking about how they have work when their friends at other dealerships don't. And somebody will say, "You know, Sewell keeps saying this customer service stuff is what's making us successful, and maybe he's right. Those other guys, who are having all those problems, don't treat the customers all that well."

Having employees help spread the word is very effective.

I've seen technicians walk over to someone new and set him straight about the way we do business. A guy may be charging two hours' labor for something that took him thirty minutes, and two or three guys will go over to him and say, "We don't do that here." If they have to talk to him a second time, they are a bit more forceful. They'll say things like, "Don't jack with our customers." And in several situations the technicians have run guys off who were mistreating our customers. They just made their lives so miserable that they quit.

At first, some people are tempted to object to our approach, because they think it will require them to work harder. But actually, in the long run, it's easier. You don't have anyone chewing on your fanny for doing work wrong, because you aren't doing it wrong.

Life is peaceful. The customer is happy. And the business is performing.

CHECKLIST

✔ *Decide to be the best.* Set your goal at the highest performance standard possible, knowing that if you expect more you're going to get more.

✔ *The boss must set the example.* The person in charge can't just preach. He has to lead by example. Leadership *is* performance. If one of your objectives is to have an immaculate facility, and you don't pick up papers in the parking lot when you see them, don't expect anybody else to do it either.

✔ *Celebrate your successes.* It will reinforce what you believe is important. Talk about your goals and values constantly. Repeatedly mention the names of people who are exceeding standards. The message will get out.

SEVEN

Every impression is important

CHAPTER 22

Selling should be theater

I love Disney World.

It's immaculate, the grounds are beautifully landscaped, and they've thought about every detail. (For example, they trim their shrubs so that they end up looking like Mickey Mouse, Dumbo, or another of their characters.)

Disney World is the image we keep in mind when we're thinking about how our stores should look. We make sure the grass is always cut. I picked out every tree and bush. And we make sure the buildings are freshly painted. We try to keep the place, both inside and out, immaculate. (We even bought a street sweeper so that we'd be able to clean the roads in front of our dealerships.)

We want our grounds to appear Disney-like.

Why devote all this attention to the grounds? Because we're setting a tone for the product we're selling. And we're setting a tone for the people who work here.

How we decorate and present our store—and a car dealership, after all, is just another kind of retail outlet—says a lot about the way we feel about our customers and employees.

And it tells people what our values are; it's in keeping with the kind of customer we want to attract. We think there's a large group of people who will want to do business with someone who appreciates flowers, trees, and landscaping.

In short, we do all this because of the message it sends. It says, "This place is different." It's not the type of automobile dealership where they play games and manners are hard to find. The message we want people to receive is that we are nice people, and this is a nice place to do business.

And the message is consistent across our entire product line. We have five dealerships. One sells Hyundais, the least expensive car on the market.

Others offer Cadillac and Lexus. Yet in each there's the same attention to detail, although the details will vary depending on the product line.

With Cadillac, for example, we try to communicate sophistication, luxury, comfort. We are selling Cadillacs; we are selling the best.

In whatever you do—whether it's the service you provide or the way you set up your office—make sure there is a "wow factor," something that will grab people's attention and make them notice that you've sweated the details.

Our interior design work was done by Tricia Wilson, a woman who has created the interiors of some of the most beautiful hotels in the world, places like St. Andrew's in Scotland, three on the grounds of Disney World in France, and the Broadmoor in Colorado Springs.

For us, she began by installing three huge Williamsburg chandeliers, then she complemented them with beautiful oak paneling throughout. All the furniture is made of mahogany, and we use leather on all chairs. Not only is it more comfortable, but we discovered it's also cheaper than fabric, because it lasts so much longer.

All this sounds simple now, but we did it wrong at first. We designed our first showroom ourselves, and customers told us it looked like we did. (They especially hated our brown vinyl furniture and chrome tables.) The difference a professional made was striking, and it really didn't cost more, given the time I saved and the fact that everything was more durable.

Today on the table in the center of the showroom is a huge vase filled with fresh flowers. That's an idea I have to thank my wife for. When Peggy and I were having dinner at La Grenouille in New York one night, she pointed out that the restaurant used fresh flowers everywhere and said they made the place feel elegant and warm at the same time. Peggy told me that if we used flowers in all of our showrooms it would probably have the same effect. She was right, and we've had flowers ever since.

The carpet has the Cadillac wreath and crest woven into it in a nice but understated way. The colors throughout are calming: soft blues and ivory. There are no signs in the windows screaming: SALE!!!

Some people argue that by decorating the dealership this way we're missing an opportunity. We aren't telling people with huge banners that we're offering 2.9% financing this week, or which car we have on special. But if our salespeople don't mention those things they're not too smart, and we don't have too many dumb salespeople.

Besides, I think most people respond better to a warm, comfortable selling environment. Again, the customer we're doing business with wants something that makes him feel more at home. You can see that in the kinds of hotels and restaurants they choose. At the Bel-Air or the Mansion at Turtle Creek, they don't have the weekend special pasted in all the windows, and when you go to 21 for lunch, you don't see "today's special" posted on a blackboard. Those places are setting a tone, and so are we.

Surprisingly, we set the tone almost exactly the same way at Hyundai—which sells cars that are a quarter the price of Cadillac or Lexus—and people seem to like it. There are some differences, of course. Since Hyundais appeal to a younger buyer, we don't have chandeliers. There's a more contemporary design with a warm, high-tech feel. The tone and style are consistent with what we're selling.

But the grounds still are immaculate, nice green grass in front, plenty of flowers, and we don't have banners hanging all over the place. This approach pays off there as well. Sales and earnings are running way ahead of projections.

At Hyundai, and at all our other stores, we do everything that we can to eliminate a high-pressure selling environment. There's always a fresh pot of coffee brewing, so we can offer you a cup, and we've even asked a local restaurant, Celebration, to open a branch at our Cadillac dealership. That way, you can get something to eat while you're waiting for your car, and our employees don't have to get their meals out of vending machines. They, like our customers, can enjoy good, healthy food.

Our idea of trying to set the right tone extends all the way to the service department. It's immaculate. The floors are scrubbed every night, and we even have a vacuum hose attached to the sander we use in the body shop. That way we capture the dust even before it hits the floor.

If we have a nice bright clean shop, the customer is going to say, "Hmmm, this place is a little different. These people must care a little bit more, and they'll probably take care of my car a little bit better."

We should do business this way. If you're going to buy a Cadillac or Lexus, your dream car, you want it to be a special experience. To some people, buying a new luxury car is like buying a loaf of bread. But there aren't many of those. For most people, spending $30,000 to $40,000 is a major event. How often do they spend that kind of money? We have to remember that although we're selling 25 new cars a day, driving home in one is still a very big deal to our customers.

Selling should be theater. We want people to see our product in an environment that makes them say, "Wow." The furniture, fixtures, lights—every detail— should contribute to making their visit to our store dramatic, entertaining, fun.

Every detail means every detail—even the places that a customer doesn't traditionally see. For example, Lexus, in designing their dealerships, included a large window that allows customers to look into the service bays. People like watching other people work. There's a little bit of sidewalk superintendent in all of us. Plus, the window tells customers we're proud of our facilities and the work we do. We want people to see what we're doing.

Some of the country's best restaurants do this. It's now not unusual to see the kitchen out in the open, and at Le Bernadin in New York they have a special table set aside that has a view of the kitchen.

This all contributes to a sense of theater.

Just to extend the analogy a bit, if selling is theater, then our selling area is the stage. We use it to set the tone. We want people to walk in and say, "Ooh!"

That's ooh, not ouch. We don't want you stumbling into a car every time you turn around. We take great pains to ensure that the showroom isn't overcrowded.

Probably the oldest expression in retailing is "You can't sell from an empty shelf," meaning you should always have plenty of merchandise on hand. And I think that's right. But just because we have plenty of inventory doesn't mean it should all be out on the showroom floor. We should have an appealing display of merchandise without appearing overcrowded, disorganized, or cluttered. The showroom should be warm and inviting.

To make sure it is, we periodically stand at our front door and look at the showroom as the customer would. We want to know whether it looks like a place where we'd feel comfortable. Does it look inviting? Is it done in good taste? Does the carpet need to be replaced? Is there anything that looks out of date?

Conversely, we also ask if there is anything in the showroom that's going to cause people to think: "I like that."

That's the reaction we're looking for. We want to get the customers' attention and have them say, "These people must care. They're concerned about the details and how their store looks." In our case it's the flowers, woodwork, and chandeliers that first catch their eye.

Can we overdo this approach? Sure. We cannot come across as pretentious. We have to be sure that the personal contact is warm and friendly and caring. If it is, people won't feel uncomfortable. We've seen people walk into the showroom, look around, and appear a little ill at ease. But if the person who comes up to them says hello, shakes their hand, thanks them for coming in, and asks what he can do to help, the customers feel welcome, and they're more likely to enjoy the experience of doing business with us.

It's important to note—at least in passing—that you can set the tone for your store in any number of different ways. Disney, for example, does it with fun. They took a state fair and turned it into theater, expensive theater. They're charging a heck of a ticket for a fair.

The point to remember is that the tone should be consistent with the product.

CHECKLIST

✔ *Look the part. Act the part.* How your business looks reflects your values and what you are selling. If you are selling a luxury product, your store should look luxurious. That doesn't mean it has to be intimidating, just tasteful. It sets a tone. Your customers will like it, and it will tacitly tell your employees how they should act. (It will also remind the boss how he should treat his employees.)

✔ *If you're not a designer, get one.* Look for experienced people. It will save you time and money.

✔ *Welcome to my home.* The easiest way to set the right tone is to think of your business as your home. You are inviting friends and neighbors in. You want them to feel comfortable.

✔ *Remember, they still charge to see a show.* The decorations and details are important to creating a sense of theater, but the merchandise is still the star. After all, no profit—no business.

Your mother was right:
manners *really* are important

W e're polite. We try to treat people—customers *and* employees—just as we treat our children, parents, spouses, or friends.

There are an awful lot of advantages that come from following what is in essence the Golden Rule. For one thing, it makes it a lot easier to go out to dinner. People don't come up and complain. Instead they say, "Gee, your people were awfully nice to us, and we sure enjoyed doing business with you."

It also makes going to work more fun. There's less conflict, because our customers like us. It's as if we're doing business with friends instead of enemies.

It's also more profitable. In the long run, creating a pleasant business atmosphere leads to higher sales and lower costs. (See Chapter 36, "This way of working really does work.")

If you want your employees to be polite to your customers, you have to be polite to your employees.

A series of little things helps create this atmosphere. For example, when a customer comes to pick up her car, the person who brings it around to her opens the door and says, "Thank you for your business. We appreciate you coming in."

When she pays her bill, the cashier hands her a little piece of chocolate, just to say thank you. (The candy helps create a pleasant feeling, just as it does in a fine hotel where they leave a chocolate on your pillow.)

If we want our customers to be treated politely, then we need to treat the people we work with politely and with respect. For example, we don't yell at customers, so we don't yell at employees.

Treating employees with respect doesn't mean you have to be weak. You can be firm without being rude. We don't have to swear at people to get them to do something. We ask politely. If that doesn't get them to do the job, we'll get someone else who will. After that happens a couple of times, everybody gets the message.

If we're going to be successful, we have to treat *everyone* like we would like to be treated. We have to, because our Cadillacs or Lexuses are no different from anyone else's. The only way we can add something to the process of buying a car is by removing the hassle (do it right the first time; free loan cars) and making the customer's life as pleasant as we know how (Saturday service; chocolates). If we can make the customer's life easier, we're rewarded.

Some of our most appreciative customers are people who've left us to buy a Jaguar, Mercedes, or BMW and have experienced the customer service those dealers provide. Once they do, they generally come back.

I have a great memory of picking up the president of a company here in Dallas who was standing out in front of the Mercedes dealership waiting for a taxi to take him to work. He needed to call a cab because he couldn't get a ride from anyone at the Mercedes dealership. I was driving down the street, and I saw him waiting there, so I picked him up and took him to his office. On the way, he shook his head and said, "I don't know why I left." Two years later, when it came time to trade in his Mercedes, he traded it to us and bought a Cadillac. He said his Mercedes was a nice car but it just wasn't worth the hassle of getting it serviced.

Since it doesn't cost anything to be nice and polite, you might wonder why everybody doesn't do business this way. In truth, I wonder too. I used to tell people the answer was simple: their mothers didn't raise them right.

But now I think it's more than that.

People are the product of where they've come from and what the values are where they work.

That last one is particularly important. The environment the boss creates says a lot about how he feels about himself and the people who work for him.

It's very rare to see a manager who treats his customers one way and his employees another. And it's awfully hard for employees to treat customers well if the boss treats them badly.

CHECKLIST

✔ *Your mother was right.* She taught you good manners—use them. Good manners never hurt anyone.

✔ *Nice is better.* Most people think being nice is the same as being weak. It isn't. It's more efficient, effective, and makes everyone feel better.

✔ *Make the extra effort.* Do the little things. Hold doors for people and carry their purchases to the car. People appreciate it. Think about how much you appreciate it when it's done for you.

CHAPTER 24

"If that's how they take care of the restrooms, how'll they take care of me?"

C lean restrooms are vital.

I probably came to this conclusion when I was a child. On our summer vacation each year we drove across the West, and I still remember how we decided at which service station to stop. We'd look at it from the outside to see if it looked clean. If it did, that meant it was likely to have clean restrooms.

But sometimes it didn't. There were several times that we stopped, and my mother, or sister, or father would walk in and find the restrooms a mess. If they did, we'd turn around and walk out—we wouldn't even stay to finish filling up the car. We'd say, "Never mind, we'll come back later. We have to go do something." Then we'd leave. Our impression of the quality of the service station was determined by the restrooms.

I think the same thing is true, to a large extent, at a car dealership or any other business.

Customers judge us on just about everything. And making sure the restroom is immaculate and tastefully decorated is another way for us to underscore our concern for them, and another way to differentiate ourselves from the competition.

Now nobody has ever said to me, "You know, I bought a car from you because your restrooms are so clean." But there have been a lot of women who've told me, "Your ladies' room is beautiful." And I've overheard people saying, "Can you believe how nice the restrooms are in this place?" That's especially important today when cleanliness in a restroom is an even more sensitive issue.

What these people are saying, when they comment about our restrooms, is that we've made an impression. It may be a little thing, but when customers are forming an opinion of you the little things add up. So we take our restrooms seriously. We use wallpaper that costs $250 a roll, something that would be found in a nice home or hotel. We hang

---

N*obody ever bought a car from us just because we had clean restrooms. But it's like the old Tom Peters line about finding coffee stains on the pull-down tray when you're on an airplane. If that's how they take care of the inside of the plane, you may get to wondering how much maintenance the engines get.*

Why would you ever want to give somebody a reason—even a subconscious reason—to question doing business with you?

---

framed prints on the walls (sports art for men; botanical drawings for women). Our floor tile has an especially high gloss, so it says clean.

Tile is rated on a scale of 1 to 4, with 4 having the highest sheen. We only use number 4 tile. It's shiny. (What I have learned, by the way, is that the cost of waxing that tile is far greater than the cost of replacing it. So while we wash it constantly—every hour on the hour—we never wax it. Instead we replace it every four years and still come out way ahead on cost.)

We also make sure that our employees' restrooms are just as nice. We learned that the hard way. We used to have a locker room for our technicians that was pretty awful, and I will never forget being at a dinner for our technicians and having our front-end tech, Sam McFarland, come over to me and say, "Carl, you may take care of your customers, but sometimes you forget about your employees. Have you looked at our restrooms? *Do you think we live like that at home?*" Well, that was humbling. A week later we had a carpenter crew in there, and we tore it out and rebuilt it and did it right.

CHECKLIST

✔ *It must be spotless*. Both the men's and women's restrooms should be cleaned hourly.

✔ *Make an impression*. There should be at least one thing in the restroom—be it the high gloss of the floor or the framed pictures on the wall—that draws attention to the fact that you've paid attention to the details.

✔ *Is the real reason there are executive restrooms* . . . because executives are afraid to go in the other ones?

CHAPTER 25

When was the last time (if ever) you thought about your signs?

Signs are a form of customer service—one that most people don't usually think about.

But they should.

Signs, after all, represent a system for telling people how to get about your store, office, or plant.

There are only three reasons for having a sign: to name your business, to describe your product, or to give directions.

If a sign doesn't accomplish one of those three functions, it should be taken down. Otherwise, what results is a visual clutter which makes your signs difficult to read. And that, of course, defeats the whole purpose of having signs in the first place.

Signs should be helpful. Most people would rather read a sign that points to the restroom than ask someone for directions. But if that sign does not exist, or it's buried among six others, it's not helping anyone.

Signs, in a subtle way, tell the world what your values are and what kind of business you are running. Since that's true, do them right.

Our signs are created by a guy named Kris Rodamer, who worked on the original signage at the Dallas-Fort Worth Airport. All of them are done in lower-case letters, because Kris showed us that makes them easier to read. He also taught us that signs should always be placed over doorways, so people know what's on the other side.

The lettering on the outside directional signs is done in the same typeface as the lettering inside. It looks better that way, more professional. It's just a little thing, but it tells you we pay attention to the details. I doubt God is in the details, but customers sure are.

As I said before, inside our dealership you won't see huge signs heralding this week's special or some wonderful deal on financing. Those kinds of banners work against what we are trying to do. We are trying to create an atmosphere where you feel at home, and most people don't have banners in their homes. We need to tell you about whatever specials are available, but we don't have to put it in the window. In fact, with the exception of discreet signs pointing out where the restrooms and fire exits are, I can't think of a reason why you'd ever want a sign in an office.

Signs say something about your organization, your thought process, your taste, your attitude toward life, what kind of person you are, and what kind of business you're running. If you have signs screaming at you from all different angles, in all different typefaces and colors, I think it suggests to customers that they are visiting a zoo or a circus, as opposed to a well-run business.

CHECKLIST

✔ *Is this sign really necessary?* Take a walk around your store and look at every sign. You'll probably find that a lot of them aren't needed. In fact, you'll probably find some that are antiques. Take them down—and sell them.

✔ *Uniformity is classy.* Make sure that the letters on all the remaining signs are the same size and have the same typeface. It's a little thing, but it tells customers that you pay attention to the details.

✔ *DON'T USE ALL UPPER CASE LETTERS.* lower case is much easier to read. no matter where you use it. (try it sometime.)

CHAPTER 26

If the boss is a crook, you can't expect the employees to be honest

People spend an awful lot of time watching what the boss does. And if the boss wants his employees to act ethically, he'd better behave that way himself. If he's dishonest in dealing with customers, employees, or even the IRS—his employees are going to think that kind of behavior is acceptable, no matter how many lectures they hear to the contrary. Even worse, good people won't work for a sleazy boss. Once they find out the boss is less than honest, they'll move on.

But even if the boss behaves ethically, how can he get the people who work for him to act the same way? Should he publish an ethics policy? Require folks to reread the Bible as a condition of employment? Hold pop quizzes on the Golden Rule?

For a long time we wrestled with how to describe an appropriate standard of behavior. Finally we got it right. We tell our people they should always ask themselves: "How would my actions appear if they were described tomorrow on the front page of the local newspaper?"

When you ask the question that way, things get real clear.

CHECKLIST

✔ *Make it clear.* Everyone should know that there is no excuse for unethical behavior.

✔ *Talking ain't enough.* The boss can't just lecture about ethics, he must show he means it by the way he acts toward everyone—employees as well as customers.

✔ *What do you do about people who violate the ethics policy?* If it's a minor breach, give them a second chance. One second chance. If it's major, fire them. Period.

CHAPTER

The only dress code you'll ever need

ere it is:

CHECKLIST

✔ *How to tell if you're appropriately dressed.* Just ask yourself, "Would I want my picture to appear in tomorrow's paper, given what I am wearing now?" (That question, which works so well for ethics, works perfectly here too.)

 If you answer no, you're wearing the wrong thing.

✔ *The rule of thumb? Be tasteful.* If you have to err, err on the side of being too conservative. Unless you are selling trendy clothing, very few people are going to be insulted by the fact that you are dressed "too" conservatively.

✔ *Uniforms are a good idea.* If they are appropriate for your business. All of our service advisers wear blue blazers, gray pants, and a tie.

EIGHT

Creating products that are easy to sell

CHAPTER

Make a little, sell a little

What do you do when the focus groups suggest an intriguing concept or you come up with an interesting idea of your own?

Try it—on a small scale.

There's a tendency to overthink things. People like to do lots of research to try to determine whether something will work. But if you listen to your customers, you'll have a feel for what they like. So why not implement the idea—on a limited basis—and see what happens? This is a lesson we borrowed from 3M. It's their approach to new products. When someone at 3M has a new idea, like Post-it notes, they make a limited sample to see who likes it, and only if it proves popular will they make more. This approach works just fine for them—and for us.

My favorite example of how this works is in Tom Peters' book, *A Passion for Excellence*. Tom tells a story about the cashier at his local liquor store. The cashier had a long line of people at his register and was real slow ringing things up. The longer it took, the more impatient Tom got. But when the guy was finally finished, he apologized for the delay and threw a couple of pieces of candy into the bag as a peace offering. It showed he really was sorry.

We liked that idea, so we bought some candy and started giving it away at the cashier window. We got a very positive reaction, so we continued doing it.

Soon after that we bought miniature copies of the Cadillac Allante from the Matchbox toy company and we gave them to kids who were in the showroom with their parents. The children's smiles—and those of their parents—told us it was a good idea. If you like kids and dogs, people think you're probably okay. And like the candy, giving away the toy cars didn't cost a lot to try, or to keep going once we saw how much people liked it.

If you want to know if an expensive program is going to work, announce it as a one-month special. That way, if it doesn't work, you're not out very much. If people like it, you can begin it in earnest the following month.

If we want to find out about larger-ticket items—such as providing free loan cars—we "try a little" by announcing the idea as a "one-month special." For example, we didn't have 257 cars when we began the free loaner program. To test the idea, we bought 5 and said everyone who brought a car in for service work during October would get a free loaner. Then we waited to see how people reacted. Customers liked the idea, and as demand increased we kept adding cars. We now have a fleet of 257 loaners.

But if people hadn't liked the idea, or it hadn't worked, we wouldn't have had to commit to it. After all, we said it was a limited-time offer.

If we are not sure about the initial reaction, we extend the "special" for another month. If at the end of two months it doesn't seem to be working, we drop it.

This "go slow" approach is something I learned the hard way. I once had what I *knew* was a great idea. I thought I had figured out a way to talk Lincoln customers into switching to Cadillac. We sent letters to every Lincoln customer in Dallas and offered them a free oil change, lubrication, and a car wash, and said we would give them a free Cadillac to drive for the day while we were doing the work. I thought it was a hell of an idea. They'd spend the day driving a Cadillac, fall in love with the car, and buy one from us.

We sent out 15,000 letters and we got two responses. I never figured out why—my guess is people thought their time was too valuable to make a separate trip for a free oil change—but I did learn one thing: never test an idea on that scale. It was an expensive lesson.

If we were to do something like that again, I'd mail 200 letters, and if that got a good response, then I'd send out the 15,000, but I'd never start with 15,000 again.

"Make a little, sell a little," also extends to the merchandise we carry. In 1989, Cadillac made a very expensive Fleetwood 60 Special, which our sales manager didn't want to stock. He said it was too expensive; nobody would buy it. But I wanted one because I thought it might sell. There are always a few people who want the best and most expensive of everything. So I asked the manager to order one for me, even though I had no intention of driving it for long. In fact, I drove it around the block and Allen Questrom (who was then chairman of Neiman-Marcus; he's now head of Federated) saw it and asked me to order one for him. If a man with that kind of taste bought one, I knew we were on to something. We sold 25 more that year.

No matter what it is, you should try a little bit of it, just to see if customers appreciate it. If it doesn't work, you're not out much.

Sometimes we forget to check to see how the idea is working once we've put it in place. We used to give away eight free oil changes with the purchase of every new car. We had that program for ten years. It sounded logical. We were giving you another reason for doing service work with us, plus it was our way of saying thank you for buying your car from Sewell Village.

Well, in 1987 business turned down, and we were trying to figure out how to cut expenses. Someone suggested we eliminate the free oil changes.

"But what happens," somebody asked, "if people get upset?"

We decided to try it for a couple of months. We figured if people missed the program we'd apologize and start it up again.

So we stopped sending out the coupons. And you know what happened? Absolutely nothing. Not one human being ever said, "Where's my free oil change certificate?" That was a surprise. It just wasn't important to our customers. Did they keep coming in for service? Yes, we still did 30 to 40 oil changes a day, usually as part of other service work. But the coupon just didn't mean very much to them. We never would have known that unless we had tried "make a little, sell a little" in reverse. We don't give free oil changes anymore.

As a result of that experience, if we're wondering whether a program we've had in place still has value, we eliminate it for a little while and see what happens.

A funny thing happened the other day. We mailed 200 free oil change certificates to Oldsmobile customers to get them to come in for service work, and we got a lot of phone calls from people saying, "What's the catch? What do I have to buy to get this?"

Nothing.

"Are you sure? I don't have to buy anything else or do anything else?"

Not a thing.

We tried it, but apparently people just don't believe that there is any such thing as a free lunch—or a free oil change.

CHECKLIST

✔ *Before you spend the big bucks* . . . try your idea on a small scale and see what happens. This concept works equally well for products, services, and pay plans.

✔ *Do everything possible to minimize your risk.* If what you want to test will cost a lot of money, introduce it as a "limited time offer." For example, you could say the program is only going to last one month. That way, you don't have to gear up for a full-blown promotion. At the end of the month you can figure out whether the program is worth continuing.

✔ *What's important to your customer today?* Just because somebody liked your idea five years ago is no guarantee that they're still going to like it today. Periodically eliminate services you are providing, and see if anybody cares. If they do, apologize and quickly put them back. If they don't, you've saved yourself some money.

CHAPTER 29

You can't give good service
if you sell a lousy product

No matter how hard you try, there's no way to provide good service if you're selling a terrible product. It will wear out too quickly or it will break. Even the best customer service system won't save you. No matter what you do, the customer is bound to be unhappy with that kind of product.

So, if you're selling a product that you think can be improved—either its quality needs upgrading, or it needs to be modified to better meet a customer's needs—you have to get that message across to the manufacturer.

Not surprisingly, that's not easy to do. After all, manufacturers think they understand their market pretty well, and besides, nobody likes to be told they could be doing a better job.

In order to get them to listen to you, you have to establish your credibility. You'll have to prove you know what you're talking about, otherwise they're going to say: "If you're all that smart, how come you can't sell what we give you?"

You establish your credibility over time. Expecting to have a great relationship and influence with your manufacturer thirty days after you sign on is unrealistic. You have to earn their trust, and that takes awhile, because you have a lot you have to prove to them. For example, you have to show that you are a good retailer. That you *can* sell what they give you. That helps your credibility no end. For example, I find I am a lot more credible with the people at Cadillac than I am at Chevrolet, because I sell a lot more Cadillacs.

But it goes beyond your performance.

First, you need to know the product cold. Nothing is going to destroy your credibility faster than suggesting that a product should be changed so that it can do X, only to find out after you've said it that it already does.

Second, you must know the market and what the competition is doing.

Third, you need to know what the development process is for your product. For example, it takes four or five years to design a totally new car. The Lexus LS 400 took seven. You need to know that before you call up demanding a new car next month, or even next year.

Finally, you need to learn to speak the manufacturer's language. That's important. Sometimes a retailer and a manufacturer will call the same thing by two different names. With cars, for instance, there's a difference between design and engineering. The designer is the person who decides how the product will look. The engineer is responsible for how it will perform. It's like putting up a building: you have an architect and an engineer. The car designer is really the architect.

And then you have to learn that manufacturing guys are different from either engineers or designers, and it takes all three to make a car. You need to know what all of them do, if you want them to pay attention.

Until you prove to the manufacturer that you really know what you're talking about, that you understand their business and problems as well as your own, they are not likely to listen to you—no matter how clever your idea.

No one is closer to the customer than the retailer. That's why it's important for them to listen to you. This—if you'll permit me a small aside—is where Cadillac has really done a great job. Cadillac's General Manager, John Grettenberger, decided when he got the job five years ago that he wanted to have dealers involved in the product development process.

So John put a group of us—dealers, engineers, manufacturing guys, and designers—in a room and he kept us there for three days. What Cadillac got, for the first time, was a useful exchange of views and information. As a result of this, dealers now understand how Cadillac does things and can make more useful suggestions about what needs to be improved. And I think the engineers and manufacturing guys now have a better understanding of our point of view as well.

When we sat down as a group, the engineers showed us that the suspension, brakes, and overall engineering on the current line of Eldorados and Sevilles were, just like the ads said, "world class." So why, they wanted to know, wasn't there a bigger demand in the marketplace for such high-quality products?

We told them that many of our customers felt there wasn't enough room inside the car, and they wanted something that looked more distinctive. As a result of those meetings, and ensuing market research (dealers, after all, are not always right), the cars are being redesigned. Cadillac is going to keep all the wonderful engineering—and even improve on it a bit—but they're going to respond to the customers' needs as well. The 1992 Eldorados, and Sevilles—the first two products to come from those meetings John Grettenberger initiated—are going to be striking. (And car buffs will be pleased to know that a completely new, 32-valve, dual overhead cam engine will be coming.)

Another advantage of having a retailer (customer, client) involved in the factory's planning process is that the retailer can say some things that are unpopular—things somebody internally might get punished or fired for saying. I have had several factory people come to me and say, "If we do this, the results would be that, and if you tell them, they might listen. You won't get shot for making the suggestion."

As a result of John's idea to get us all together, we now have a program that encourages top managers from Cadillac to come to a dealer's showroom and talk to customers, so they can learn first hand what's going on. John has created lines of communication that had never existed in all of Cadillac's history.

Maybe in the past we didn't need to have everyone involved. But now we do. Today, it seems, every marketplace is extremely competitive. We have to stay close to the customer to find out exactly what kind of product he wants. That means we must involve everybody who deals with customers in the planning process.

The easiest way to make sure your ideas are acted on is to start by suggesting easy wins: ideas that can be accomplished with very little effort but are bound to have a big payoff.

For example, when the Allante first came out, customers liked it a lot, but they kept telling us they wished the car came in either red or black, two colors that weren't offered. Dealers passed that information on to Cadillac.

Now adding colors to a line is not that hard—or expensive—to do. Cadillac listened, added the colors, and now half of the Allantes sold are either black or red.

So, first, you establish your credibility with easy wins. Then, once you've proven you know what you're talking about, you go after more ambitious things, like trying to get them to double the engine's horsepower, or having Cadillac enter Formula One Grand Prix racing circuit.

But whether you are talking about an easy win or something harder, you always make your suggestions politely, and you always present them from the manufacturer's point of view. John Sewell had a wonderful description of that. He called it the "you viewpoint." That's as old as the hills, but it's still a wonderful idea. Does your idea help them? If it helps them, it's an easier sell. To expect people not to work for their own self-interest is pretty naive.

Given that, what we try to say is: "This idea will help sell more cars. That's something we both want. So could we give the idea a try? I think it will work."

But we have to be right. People really must want black and red added to the line. If what you say is true, they'll continue to listen to you. But if what you said turned out to be wrong—especially if it was the first or second time you suggested something—they'll quit listening.

How do we decide what to suggest? That's easy. We listen to our customers. We talk to them, and we also spend a bunch of time with our salespeople. After all, they're the ones who are closest to our customers. And we talk to people who used to be our customers. (Like every good business, we try to stay in touch with our customers.) We want to know why they bought a new Mercedes instead of a Cadillac or a Lexus.

Once you have that information, you need to find the right person to give it to. This is important. If your contact at the plant is receptive, that's great. If not, look for someone who is, and it may not be the department head. It might be somebody two levels down. You may have to find the person who is on the way up and is trying to make a difference. Your idea may mean another step up the corporate ladder for him.

The easiest way to find the right person is to send up a trial balloon, as they say in Washington. When someone grabs one and says, "I like that," then you know you have the person who is going to champion your idea within the company.

But you're never going to get anywhere unless your idea is right. Credibility, credibility, credibility. You have to have that. You have to be 100% convinced that you're right. You don't have to survey 9,000 people who tell you they want black and red. Maybe it's 90. But you must have information that is convincing to the manufacturer. You have to sell them. The process is no different than selling your customers.

This is not going to happen overnight. Remember, you are building your credibility, and that can only happen over time, because people will want to evaluate you. Do you have a genuine caring concern for the company whose product you're selling, or are you some kind of transient opportunist who will sell the hot product for a while and then just move on?

While they're deciding, the clock will keep ticking. There's no way around it. In the short run, you probably could make a little more money by staying home and trying to sell more of the product you have. But in the long run, if you help your supplier produce a better product, one that is more desirable to the customer, you'll make more money. Since the customer service race is a marathon, not a sprint, that approach makes more sense.

CHECKLIST

✔ *Make it easy for them to hear you.* Most manufacturers think they understand their markets. They're not necessarily going to want to hear there's room for improvement. To get them to listen—really listen—you'll have to prove that you understand and care about their problems and processes as well as your own.

✔ *Build credibility.* Don't hip-shoot. If you want the manufacturer to act on your suggestions, those suggestions have to be right. Don't go to them with guesses or hunches. Show them you care enough to invest your time and money to come up with evidence that proves your point.

✔ *Go for the easy ones.* Make sure your first suggestion is something inexpensive that will produce results right away. Get a series of small victories under your belt before you start talking about the need for the manufacturer to redo his entire product line.

✔ *Great relationships, like great wine . . .* get better over time. This entire process of building a relationship with the manufacturer is going to take a while. You can't rush it, so don't expect miracles.

NINE

Borrow, borrow, borrow

CHAPTER 30

Why reinvent the wheel?
Just improve it

Whenever we want to try something that's new for us, we look around to see how other people have handled it. Why reinvent the wheel, when there are other people who've already figured out the best way to do it?

It just makes sense to learn how other people have done things, and then modify their approach to fit your circumstances.

Here's one way we did that. One of the things I hate about car dealerships is that they always have loudspeakers blaring the name of someone somebody is trying to find. It's annoying and unprofessional, but I didn't know what to do about it until I wandered into a pizza place.

I had taken my kids to Chuck E. Cheese—that's the pizza chain where they have singing and dancing animals, rides, and loads of Nintendo video games. If you want something to eat, you walk up to the counter and place your order. Then you go watch the show, or put the kids on the rides, until your food is ready.

Given the noise in that place—the "animatronic" animals, the games, the screaming kids—there is no way for somebody to yell, "Sewell, your pizza's done." You'd never hear them.

Here's how they handle it. After you've placed your order, they give you a number—just as they do at the supermarket deli counter. Then, every time an order is done, a pleasant-sounding chime goes off. That's your signal to look at the TV monitors they've put all over the place. Every time an order is ready, the corresponding number comes up on the monitors.

The system works just fine. Nobody has to yell, and the customers don't have to mill around the kitchen door, wasting time, waiting for their food.

I thought that was a heck of an idea. So we borrowed it and modified it a bit.

What used to happen at our dealerships was that you'd pay your bill and the cashier would pick up a microphone and say, "Please bring up car number 473." Upon hearing the announcement, one of the customer service reps was supposed to go search the lot, find your car, and bring it around front for you.

The system never worked very well. First, the announcements blared all day long. Second, we were never sure if the reps heard the page. They might have been inside another car, with the windows rolled up, or on the phone, or somebody might have been talking to them. The only way we really knew that they got the message was if they brought the car around. If they didn't, the customer waited, and waited, and waited, and would eventually complain. When he did, we'd make the announcement again, and the whole process would start all over.

That was no way to provide customer service.

Today—thanks to Chuck E. Cheese—here's what happens when you pay your bill: The cashier enters that information into a computer, and it also shows up on a computer monitor on the service drive. When they see it, a service rep logs on and says he's going to get the car, and that information is relayed back to the cashier. If the service rep doesn't log on, we know something is wrong, and someone is sent to find out what the problem is.

With the new system, there are no loudspeaker announcements, and we always know whether or not the car is on the way up. More important, the average time of delivering the car to the customer has been cut from six minutes to two. All of these improvements can be traced directly back to our visit to the local pizza place.

We borrow ideas every chance we get, because it just makes so much sense. Why would we want to figure out a problem on our own, when somebody has already done it for us? Sometimes you don't have any choice, of course. In some situations, what you want to do is unique. But that's pretty rare. Most times you can borrow a solution. Bill Marriott is going to know a hell of a lot more about systems that can handle large numbers of people quickly and efficiently than I am ever going to know. So why shouldn't I benefit from his expertise?

Why shouldn't you take the best ideas McDonald's, American Airlines, and Disney have to offer and see how they can be modified to fit your business? We have. Repeatedly. (That's one of the reasons Tom Peters' books are so popular. He shows you how the best companies do things.)

We're already talked about how we want our facility to be Disney-like. We found out what kind of tile McDonald's uses in its restaurants, and now it's the only kind we'll use in our service areas. If it can stand up to

Books are a never-ending source of ideas to borrow. Here are a baker's dozen of my favorites.

Berry, Leonard L., Parasuraman, A., Zeithaml, Valarie A. *Delivering Quality Service*. New York: The Free Press.

Bradshaw, Pete. *Personal Power*. Englewood Cliffs: Prentice-Hall, Inc.

Cusumano, Michael A. *The Japanese Automobile Industry*. Cambridge: The Harvard University Press.

Deming, W. Edwards. *Out of the Crisis*. Cambridge: Massachusetts Institute of Technology, Center for Advanced Engineering Study.

Goldratt, Eliyahu M., Cox, Jeff. *The Goal*. Croton-on-Hudson: North River Press.

Marcus, Stanley, *Minding the Store*. Boston: Little, Brown and Company.

————. *Quest for the Best*. New York: The Viking Press.

Ohno, Taiichi. *Workplace Management*. Cambridge: Productivity Press.

Ohno, Taiichi, Setsuo, Mito. *Just-in-Time for Today and Tomorrow*. Cambridge: Productivity Press.

Peters, Tom. *Thriving on Chaos*. New York: Alfred A. Knopf.

Peters, Thomas J., Waterman, Robert H., Jr. *In Search of Excellence*. New York: Harper & Row.

Shingo, Shigeo. *A Study of the Toyota Production System from an Industrial Engineering Viewpoint*. Cambridge: Productivity Press.

Sloan, Alfred P., Jr. *My Years with General Motors*. New York: Doubleday/Currency.

the foot traffic at a McDonald's, it's going to be strong enough to hold up in our service department. And we modeled our sales incentives after American's AAdvantage program.

If an idea works in one place, you can be pretty certain it will work in another. People are just not that different from one another.

We found borrowing ideas to be so effective that we organize field trips to find new ones. Our body shop technicians went to California to see how they make repairs out there. The department manager went to see the best body shops in Europe to learn how they do such a wonderful job in matching the paint on cars that come in for repairs. As a result we now use Sikkens paints, and Garmat paint booths.

We also shop our competitors. That can be a tremendous help because you can see what they're up to. I'll drive by their showrooms on a Sunday, just to see how they're displaying their merchandise. And we will have a couple of people we're sure they won't recognize buy cars from them, so we can find out how they handle customers, what their prices are and, in general, see what we can learn from them. (As a result of this program, we started using one of our competitor's banks to provide financing to our customers. Chase was providing much better terms than the bank we had been using.)

Other times we go someplace that has nothing to do with us—like a restaurant, hotel, amusement park, or museum—to see what they are doing in terms of service, uniforms, lighting, or music.

When I talk to people about this—how we borrow whenever we can—they sometimes say, "That's really nice for you down there in Dallas, but my customers here in New York (or Chicago, San Francisco, or wherever) are different, and it will never work for us."

Well, there is an old Texas saying that really applies to that. Bullshit. There's absolutely nothing that aggravates me more than to hear people say, "It won't work where I live."

A lot of the good systems and programs we have, we borrowed from somebody else, and those somebody elses were located all over the map. All those ideas worked in Dallas and they'll work in Philadelphia, New York, Los Angeles, or anywhere else. After all, they even worked in New Orleans.

Now New Orleans is a very different city than Dallas. And people said our way of doing business wouldn't work there, because people in New Orleans are more demanding, and tougher on a buck. But our approach to doing business there—we have a Cadillac and Chevrolet dealership in New Orleans—worked just fine. People like good service, no matter where they live.

The best systems work everywhere. And if you don't have them, find the companies that do, and adapt them to fit your business.

CHECKLIST

✔ *Borrow. It's quicker.* Given enough time, you'll be able to figure out just about anything. But why waste that time? When confronted with a new problem, look around to see how other people have handled it.

✔ *Borrow from the best.* Once you've decided to borrow ideas, borrow from the pros. Who does the best job of maintaining their facilities? Disney, of course. So they became our model when we thought about how our grounds should look. The tile on our service department drive is made by the same people who supply McDonald's. We figured they visited every tile manufacturer on earth, so we didn't have to.

✔ *Actively search for ideas to borrow.* Organize field trips to go look for new ideas. If you see an idea you like, ask about it. People love to talk about their business.

✔ *Don't be afraid to tinker.* We don't have a monorail running through the middle of our dealerships, and we don't have thousands of people staying with us each night, all of whom want to get up at 7 A.M. Yet we have used Disney ideas about cleanliness and Marriott's systems for handling large numbers of people. Modify the ideas you borrow to fit your circumstances.

CHAPTER 31

"The things you don't know
are the history you haven't read"

"The things you don't know are the history you haven't read." Harry Truman used to say that. Our consultants—Stanley Marcus, Steve Mulvany, and Tom Peters—are invaluable because they teach us that history. When we need to borrow ideas in a more systematic way, we use consultants, both formal ones and informal ones. Because they've been places we've never seen, and spent time with successful people we've never met, they're able to offer ideas we might never have come up with.

If we end up feeling comfortable with a consultant, we tend to keep the relationship going for a long time. The longer we work together, the better they know our business, and the more valuable they become.

Pete Bradshaw is a great example of that. When we first met him, he was teaching organizational behavior at a seminar Cadillac sponsored at Harvard, and he didn't know much about selling, servicing, and fixing cars. But he's learned, and he has taken his knowledge about our business and added to it the things he has observed in consulting with oil companies, airlines, and publishing companies.

Specifically, he's shown us that people who feel good about themselves and what they are doing will do a better job of taking care of the customer.

Let Bradshaw tell you.

> When we—you, me, everybody—genuinely approve of ourselves, we can afford to be responsive to the needs and wants of others. People who feel powerless, or who don't think they are valued, don't care much about the problems of others.

The secret, says Bradshaw, is to create an environment in which people feel they're important to the company's success. He feels there are four components that allow that self-esteem to prosper.

They are a sense of:

1 *Achievement*. The person's work is objectively measured against clear and fair goals that are directly tied to compensation and advancement.

2 *Being cared about*. Conditions at work clearly demonstrate respect and concern for each person in the organization.

3 Power. The company encourages individuality and autonomy consistent with agreed-upon standards and values. Everyone is expected to propose better ways of doing things. All suggestions, whatever their source, are taken seriously. Just about anyone who cares to can have a significant influence over how things are done.

4 *Ethics and values*. Ethical standards must be clear, stringently enforced, and consistent. In recruiting, every effort is made to find people with similar values. Those who violate the standards are fired.

As you can see, we've used Bradshaw's ideas to help us build our dealerships.

Another role he has assumed is that of father confessor. There are just some things you can't discuss with people you work with every day. If you're thinking about selling the company; if you're thinking about firing somebody who's been with you a long time; if you're thinking about bringing in a new top executive—it's probably better to talk those things through with someone who is a disinterested—knowledgeable, but disinterested—third party than it is to talk about them with a member of your staff.

Pete also serves in this role for other people in our company. People can go to him and say, "I'm having a helluva problem with Carl, or with my manager," and Pete doesn't throw them under a bus. He shows them how to resolve the problem. In addition, he conducts our annual round table discussion at which all of our managers get together to talk about problems and opportunities we have at all our dealerships.

Pete does all this in addition to serving as a sounding board for me. I don't always take his advice, but even when I don't his ability to make me look at an issue from a different angle is invaluable.

For example, Stanley Marcus talks to us all the time about the need to see things from the customer's perspective. Thanks to him, we know all the wonderful systems we put in place won't mean a thing unless the customer benefits.

When Stanley retired as chairman of Neiman-Marcus, I asked if I could hire him as a consultant. He smiled and said, "Carl, you can't afford me." And he was absolutely right. I couldn't afford him as a full-time consultant. But he suggested we have lunch once a month and that reduced the fee enough to where it was something I could afford. That's how what

Harry Truman was right when he said "The things you don't know are the history you haven't read." In searching for people to draw on in building your business look for people who were there when that history was being written. They just might have the perspective—and insight— you need.

has turned into an absolutely wonderful relationship began. What a history he has to draw upon! Stanley has a perspective on retailing that no one else has. One of the things he has taught me is that quality and value will always win out. Whoever has the best goods is going to be the person the consumer seeks out. Over time, if you have the best car, and provide the best service, the customers will find you. The good guys really do win in the end.

And if you have good guys as consultants, you'll win too.

CHECKLIST

✔ *You are still running the business.* While you should use consultants, don't substitute their opinion for your own. If you do what you feel in your gut is right, you'll be better off ninety-nine times out of a hundred. But use consultants to get ideas, and as sounding boards.

✔ *Experience can be a good teacher.* When picking a consultant, or just looking for someone to talk to about your business, try to find people with experience and a history of success. They've probably already gone through—and solved—many of the problems you're wrestling with.

✔ *Build a relationship.* Once you have found good consultants, stick with them. Good consultants get better over time, because the more they know about you and your organization, the more they have to offer.

TEN

You are the message

CHAPTER 32

Speak softly but . . .

We have two simple goals when we sit down to create an ad: we want it to truly reflect the way we do business, and we want it to be something we're proud to show our family and friends.

In other words, we want it to be consistent with everything else we do around here.

As we go about creating our advertising, we always remember what it is we want our company to stand for. Together with our ad agency—Dallas-based Puskar, Gibbon and Chapin—we have come up with a simple statement that clearly communicates our goal: "The Sewell dealerships will always operate with dignity, integrity, and style, while consistently offering the best customer service in the areas in which we compete."

That gave us a foundation on which to build our ads. Often we tell a simple story, and we almost always use music to set the tone for our radio spots.

We're consistent in what we say—stressing one thing one week and something else the next just confuses people—and we're specific.

You'll get the idea, if you look at some of the radio spots we use.

ANNCR: Sewell Village Cadillac has asked Mr. Stanley Marcus to discuss service.

MARCUS: Somerset Maugham once wrote, "It's a funny thing about life, if you refuse to accept anyhing but the best you very often get it." As a merchant, I've discovered that people who expect the best merchandise also expect the best service. Once they find it, they have very little reason to shop anywhere else.

ANNCR: For over 70 years, the Sewell family has catered to people who expect the best from an automobile and a service department. Through our dedication to service we've grown into the largest Cadillac dealer in the Southwest with a service department

	open all day Saturday plus 150 free loan cars, convenient service reservations, and most important, personal attention.
MARCUS:	Once you establish excellent service, you provide a safe harbor to which customers can always return.
ANNCR:	Sewell Village Cadillac, Lemmon Avenue at University.

SFX:	MUSIC UP AND UNDER. STREET SOUNDS AND SOUNDS OF OLD-TIME CARS AND HORNS.
ANNCR:	It's 1911. Hemlines are up, families are in, and America is in love with that new invention, the automobile. Seeing the opportunity, the Sewell family began selling cars. They base their business on one simple belief: Always treat the customer the way you would want to be treated. Over the years, this belief would be passed on and grow into a family of six dealerships.
SFX:	STREET SOUNDS AND SOUNDS OF MODERN CARS.
	It's 1990. Hemlines are up, families are in, America is in love with the automobile, and every Sewell dealership is still based on one simple belief: Always treat the customer the way you would want to be treated. Sometimes, the more things change, the more they remain the same.
	Sewell Village Cadillac-Sterling, Sewell Oldsmobile, Sewell Buick-Hyundai, and Sewell Lexus. A family tradition of service since 1911.
SFX:	MUSIC UP AND OUT.

Hopefully, these ads will also sell the product, but I don't think there's ever a good argument for doing hard-sell advertising or creating ads that will mislead the customer. They may work for a year, but those types of ads won't pay off in the end. If there's a way to have a little touch of class in your advertising, it makes you stand out above all the gimmicky, noisy ads. Those kinds of ads make me uncomfortable. We don't yell around the dealership, so we shouldn't yell in our ads.

While you want your ads to sell product, remember that your ads are also a reflection of who you are.

When we do talk, we don't go on about how we have the best service in town, and how warm and caring our people are. Everybody does that, even when it isn't true, and customers just don't believe those kinds of claims anymore.

Instead of telling, we try to show them. In most of our ads we manage to work in free loan cars and Saturday service. Those tangible examples communicate what we are all about. And then when the customers experience our service and realize we do treat them well (and do the job right the first time), it's the icing on the cake. It's the clincher to get them to come back.

CHECKLIST

✔ *Classy.* Businesses that try to compete by always having the lowest price eventually go broke. Don't feel compelled to talk about price in your ads. Instead, try to communicate what you're really all about.

✔ *Show, don't tell.* The specific beats the general every time. Don't say you have the friendliest people. Give examples of what they've done, or will do, for customers. Let the customers conclude that you have the best service in town.

✔ *You are the message.* With everything we do, we're sending a message, to both our customers and our employees, about what kind of place we're running and what we think is important. So the details count, whether it's the clothes we wear, or the language we use, or the kind of writing paper we choose.

✔ *Take the time to read the most current ratings book and circulation.*
1 Radio—Arbitron
2 TV—A.C. Nielsen
3 Magazines—Simmons Market Research Bureau
4 Newspapers—Scarborough Newspaper Ratings Co.

This stuff is not nuclear physics, no matter what the media buyer may say.

Promotions:

wet T-shirts or the symphony?

Our promotions, like our advertising, are designed to build a relationship with our customers. When customers think of Sewell Lexus or Sewell Village Cadillac, we want them to have a clear (and hopefully positive) image in mind. Our promotions also give us a chance to give our business a personality.

As I was growing up in Dallas, Neiman-Marcus was *the* store—it set the retail standard for the entire state of Texas. It carried the best merchandise, its sales staff was the most helpful, and you knew if you ever had a problem with anything you bought they'd take it back. No questions asked. But Stanley Marcus also decided that his business should stand for fun. That's why they offer the annual extravagant Christmas presents each year.

We got to thinking about how Neiman-Marcus created its image—and how automobile dealers don't engender particularly warm feelings among the general populace—and we decided our promotions should show people that we're not your average car dealer.

We started by inviting our customers to an annual party at which we'd introduce the new cars for that year. We served champagne, roast beef, and elaborate desserts. We hired a band, dressed all our managers and salespeople in black tie, and in general made a big deal about showing off the new cars. We didn't try to sell any of our guests a car—although, if they twisted our arm, we would. We just wanted to celebrate the beginning of the new car season and to thank our customers for having done business with us in the past.

That was the beginning, and then every year after that we'd try to do something a little more elaborate. We had Larry Hagman help us open our Cadillac dealership when we moved to our new location. That was during the summer of *Who Shot J.R.?* and more than 5,000 people showed up to see him.

(We had invited all of our customers, but then word got out and it seemed like everyone was calling to see if they could meet "J.R." We finally decided to open it up to anyone who showed up driving a Cadillac. People came from all over the state. We had room to park five or six hundred cars and that was nowhere near enough. People were paying the neighbors who lived around the dealership to park in their yards, the way they do at football games. It was wonderful.)

Promotions draw attention to you. Make sure every detail is right. Otherwise, people will walk away with the wrong impression, which is far worse than what would have happened if you hadn't held the promotion at all.

We've had Western art exhibits from the Cowboy Hall of Fame, and we've had the local Model Railroad Association construct exhibits so that all the dads could bring their kids to see the trains, or the kids could bring their dads. We're not sure which. And since everyone loves great food, we frequently try to invite a great chef. In addition to having Paul Prudhomme cook for us at our dealerships in Dallas and New Orleans we've also had Texas' legendary chef Don Strange.

Now all of this draws attention to the dealership, but that's really not the primary reason for the promotions. First, we want to thank people for their business. That's important because you can't thank your customers enough. And second, and this is the real reason, we're trying to build a relationship with our customers and give them yet another reason to do business with us.

CHECKLIST

✔ *Every promotion tells a story—or should.* Sure, promotions are fun and attract attention, but you might also think about what effect they'll have on your company's overall image. Sponsoring the local symphony says one thing. Holding a wet T-shirt contest says another.

✔ *When in doubt, just invite your old customers.* Inviting prospective clients to a ball game or some other event is as American as apple pie. But don't take current customers for granted. They're the reason you're still around.

✔ *Do it right.* A promotion, by definition, is a big event. Don't cut corners. Make it a black tie affair. Hire a band. Fill the place with fresh flowers. Bear in mind that you are trying to create an impression that will be remembered. Would you rather have people recall that you served flat soda and stale pretzels, or champagne and crab cakes?

ELEVEN

Bring 'em back alive

CHAPTER 34

The $332,000 customer

As you have seen, I believe in manners, saying please and thank you, sir and ma'am. Is there a payoff in being polite? In having a nice showroom? In treating people with respect? You bet. In the long run, we will do more business because we take care of our customers and their problems.

Will this way of doing business appeal to everybody?

No.

Are there people who are always going to be looking for the last dollar?

Yes.

That kind of person might enjoy going to Sears and buying his own oil filter, and then going to K Mart to get the oil on special. Then, convinced he has saved seven whole dollars, he happily crawls under his car and changes the oil and filter himself. He'll beat our price, but he'll spend three hours doing it.

How much could a person spend with you in the course of a lifetime? That's the question we ask every time we meet with a customer. You don't want to deal with somebody just once; you want his business forever. We don't want to sell a customer just one car, but ten or twenty in coming years.

Are we going to make an extra effort for someone who might buy twenty cars from us? You bet.

But most people have better things to do with their time than spend three hours changing their oil. They want as much hassle as possible removed from their lives. When they shop, they want a pleasant environment, and we want to give it to them, not because we want to sell them one automobile, but so that we have a chance to sell them ten or twenty. That's the number of cars they'll buy in a lifetime, and it adds up to a lot of money. If cars are $25,000 apiece, 12 cost $300,000. Then you have the parts and service work that go on top of it. It adds up to be a substantial number, in our case $332,000. Every time you get a chance to sell a customer one item—be it a pack of gum or a car— you need to think about how much he represents in future business.

There is also the rock-in-the-pool theory to explain why you should treat customers this way. When we do a real good job for customers, they tell their friends. That word-of-mouth advertising is stronger than anything we can do on television. In fact our advertising line is, "Ask the person who drives one." If people will ask our customers about what it's like to do business with us, we have a much better chance of getting them to become customers themselves.

And every car we can sell to a friend represents another potential $332,000 in business.

So you can see that, while I truly believe in treating customers as you would a spouse, parent, or friend, it's not all altruism. We are all motivated by self-interest. We do think about "What's in it for me?" And if we treat people in a positive, comfortable way, we're going to do more business than if we rough them up and bounce them around. The folks who feel comfortable roughing them up don't care if the customer comes back.

Now there are places like Sears, where, when you walk in the door, you know not to expect a lot of service. You're there for one reason, and that's price. But that's not why we're in business. We're trying to provide a warm, enjoyable experience, like going to a fine hotel. You're willing to pay a little more because they treat you so nice, and there's that piece of chocolate on the pillow, and the shower is not two drops a minute but comes out full force when you turn it on, and the towels are big and fluffy.

The cost of providing this kind of environment adds to our cost—but it also adds to our volume. So, while our margins are not as great as some people's, the money we take to the bank is. Why? Because we take care of our customers, and they come back and bring their friends. As a result, we think we'll be in business for a long, long time.

CHECKLIST

✔ *Don't play them one at a time.* Don't look at customers as people who make a purchase and then disappear forever. Do everything in your power to make the first experience of dealing with you—and every subsequent one—as pleasant as possible. If you do, they'll come back. If you need to be motivated, think about all the money that customer could spend with you in the course of a lifetime.

✔ *Keep score.* You should know who your $332,000 customers are and treat them accordingly. While you are going to be nice to everybody, these people should get extra attention. They should never have to wait—or want—for anything.

✔ *What are you really selling?* Most people are buying solutions, not products. And often they'll be happy to trade money for (more) time.

CHAPTER 35

How to be forgiven your trespasses

If you treat people right, they'll forgive your mistakes—at least once, maybe twice.

Now this isn't automatic. It's much like a bank account. Every time we do our job right the customer credits our account. Every time we make a mistake he debits it—but one debit tends to equal ten credits. As long as we have a positive balance, the customer will probably forgive us.

That's a big deal. Think about all the times you've gone to a new restaurant only to find the service was poor or the food bad. Odds are you didn't go back. You had no reason to. You didn't have any kind of relationship worth continuing.

Everything you need to know about handling mistakes you learned in nursery school: acknowledge your error, fix it immediately, and say you're sorry. Odds are, your customers, like your mom and dad, will forgive you.

But, hopefully, we've given you a reason to keep coming back, even if we err. Maybe you remember that we've always been polite and done the job right in the past. Or that the service adviser always remembered the kind of oil you wanted us to use when we tuned up your car and knew you really would shoot any technician who smoked while working inside your car.

You remember that we care and that we try hard. So if we make a mistake you'll tend to forgive us.

The goal is never to disappoint a customer. But if you've built a relationship with your customer, you can really stumble badly once and still be okay.

CHECKLIST

✔ *You've built up a certain amount of good will* . . . don't blow it now. If you're wrong—or the customer thinks you are—admit it right there, and solve the problem.

✔ *You don't have to buy people off.* A *sincere* apology and correcting the problem immediately should almost always take care of the problem.

✔ *Don't make it a habit.* Having a long history of providing good service is what allows the customer to forgive you. Don't take advantage of his good nature by making a second mistake.

CHAPTER

This way of working
really does work

"*I*chiban" works.

I think our track record proves our approach to customer service leads to a more profitable business. Intuitively, when we explain our approach to people, they understand why it works. They say something like: "Sure, if you treat me right, I'm more likely to buy from you and keep buying from you."

Most people say that. Most, but not all. There are some folks for whom this is all too touchy-feely.

Well, I got tired of those people saying we were wasting money by spoiling our customers. They said our success stemmed from some kind of luck. So we asked J. D. Power and Associates—that's the independent research firm well known for evaluating car quality—to evaluate us. They surveyed our customers—without telling anyone who they were working for—to find out how we were doing. I was hoping their report might produce some hard numbers that proved we were on the right track with our customer service approach, as well as point out places where we could do better.

The results were gratifying. Who wouldn't want the recognized experts in their field saying the following about their business: "Sewell Village Cadillac is doing an exemplary job in satisfying its customers. Its extremely positive 'people' evaluations are the strength of the dealership."

"*If* Sewell Village Cadillac were included as a nameplate in the [study], its score would tie it with this year's first place finisher, Acura."

That was the way the report opened. Dave Power went on to say that our customer service scores were 31.5% better than the national average, and that our people were outstanding. For example, they outscored Cadillac nationally by 45% for service adviser excellence, and Cadillac was the highest rated domestic nameplate.

There was more good news, like the following table:

PERCENT RATING DEALER SERVICE FACILITY EXCELLENT FOR:	Sewell	Cadillac national average	Tops Cadillac national average by
Courtesy extended to customers	84%	54%	56%
Ease of obtaining appointment	75	54	39
Helpfulness of service personnel	75	49	53
Knowledge of service personnel	66	42	57

Again, our people did very well—just about everyone who didn't rate them as "excellent" gave them a "very good."

"It is hard to imagine that dealership evaluations can get any better," Power wrote, adding that our customer satisfaction scores were just as good as Acura's, which ranked number one in Power's study of customer satisfaction.

Still, I didn't think we had the information to silence the skeptics.

And then I found it.

The survey asked two questions that go to the heart of whether or not good customer service leads to higher sales.

Power asked our customers, and those at other Cadillac dealerships nationwide, if they were "very satisfied" with the car they bought. It's an intriguing question, because the cars we get are no different from the ones that go to anyone else.

Yet even though the cars are the same, our "very satisfied" score was 25% higher than the national average. *Our customers thought more of the car because of the way we treated them before and after the sale.*

If that's true, you'd expect us to get more repeat customers than other dealers, and Power, as you can see on the next page, found that's true.

So what this study shows is that we weren't wasting our money by spoiling our customers.

This way of doing business feels good. More important, it really does work.

PERCENT WHO INDICATED THEY WOULD/WOULD NOT PURCHASE THE SAME MAKE	Sewell	Cadillac nationwide
Definitely would	47%	35%
Probably would not	9	13
Definitely would not	3	9

CHECKLIST

✔ *Have outsiders take a look.* While you will be surveying your customers on a regular basis, you still should have an expert come in periodically, say every three years, to see how you're doing. Not only will that let you double-check that your surveys are right, but the expert will be able to tell you how you're doing compared to others nationwide.

✔ *Look for the good—and bad.* You certainly want the consultant to find things that need improving, but don't forget to make a big deal out of the things they find you are doing right.

✔ *Thank you.* I hope you found some ideas you can use.

Afterword
by Stanley Marcus

What you've just finished reading is something you don't find in too many books—common sense, plainly stated.

The author, Carl Sewell, has the ability to define problems and reduce them into simple components which can then be solved. Above all, he has the capacity to think straight. He writes as he talks, and he talks as he thinks.

In this book, he explains how he engaged me as a consultant, but he doesn't relate the whole story. My reply to his invitation was that I knew so little about automobiles that I doubted if I could be of much help to him. His reply was that he didn't need to learn about cars, but more about running a business selling luxury products.

Carl realized that the only exclusivity he could ever possess in the automobile business was a superior quality of service, and he set out to build it with zeal and imagination and common sense.

Recently I addressed a group of European industrialists who had come to the United States to study how some American firms have achieved such high service standards. I told them that first of all they had to respect their customers; second, they had to learn to love them; eventually they would adore them.

All of this is what Carl Sewell knows so well and has put to work with such sincerity. It's so simple that it might appear miraculous that so few have copied his techniques. Carl really cares, and that is the hardest thing of all to copy. From reading *Customers for Life*, it's evident that Carl's mother "raised him right."

Not only is this the definitive textbook for anyone in automobile manufacturing or selling, but it is equally valid for everyone engaged in the process of selling to the ultimate customer.

If you don't learn from this book, it's your fault.

Acknowledgments
(Our heroes and heroines)

BACKSTAGE (*Actually, they create the stage.*): Barbara Bouyea, Jud Chapin, Roger Crownrich, Jim Gibbon, Brock Hannan, Connie Jackson, Stan Carman, Scooter Galt, John Littlefield, Bob Obele, Don Powell, Ross Puskar, Bill Reed, Jim Rimelspach, Gale Sliger, John Stallings, Harry Wallis, Captain White, Trisha Wilson, Beth Wright.

CADILLAC: (*These are the people who have taken time to help me, but most important, they are the people who care deeply about Cadillac and have contributed so much to its rebirth.*) Gary Cowger, John Deere, Bob Dorn, Bill Flynn, Pete Gerosa, John Grettenberger, Warren Hirschfield, Tim Jones, Jerry Kitzmiller, Jim Kornas, Peter Levin, Bill Lewellen, Frank Liebgott, Alex Morton, Dave Nottoli, Karl Pierce, Jeff Pritchard, Braz Pryor, Rosetta Riley, Dick Ruzzin, Steve Seaton, Ellie Torre, Dick Welday, Dee Wood.

FRIENDS (*Who contributed to the book*): Wick Allison, Ken Batchelor, Berry Cash, Al Casey, Baron Cass, Handley Dawson, Jr., Hank Faulkner, Jerry Ford, A. T. Higgins, Alen Hollomon, Ray Hunt, Taka Inayama, Erik Jonsson, Jack Knox, Bernie Kraft, Stanley Marcus, Ted McLaughlin, Bob Moore, Roger Penske, Ross Perot, Bill Piercy, Hal Quinley, Leonard Riggs, Doug Shamburger.

GENERAL MOTORS (*I owe the following people my everlasting thanks. They know why.*): J. T. Battenberg, Dick Bugno, Keith Crutcher, Dennis Dreyer, Mike Grimaldi, Bill Hogland, Don Hudler, Skip LeFauve, Dennis Little, Mike Losh, Larry Lyons, Bud Moore, Jim Perkins, Knox Ramsey, Lloyd Reuss, Pat Roberts, Sue Scheuermann, Ed Schreitmueller, Gary Sigman, Jack Smith, Bob Starr, Bob Stempel, Tom Stephens, Dale Sullivan.

LEXUS (*These people did it right the first time, and epitomize "the relentless pursuit of perfection."*): Mack Arai, Dick Chitty, Scott Gilbert, Hiro Hatanaka, Dave Illingworth, Akio Kamiya, Bob McCurry, Don Stephenson, Steven Tolerico, Yukiyasu Togo, Tetsuro Toyoda, Mindy Weiman-Geller, Dean Workman.

TEACHERS: Len Berry, Pete Bradshaw, Edwards Deming, Eliyahu Goldratt, Pauline Graivier, Wayne Hawkins, Stanley Marcus, Steve Mulvany, Mike Nichols, Taiichi Ohno, Tom Peters, Les Silver, Genichi Taguchi, Jack Williams.

I don't know how to categorize these folks, but they have helped a lot: Larry Adams, Ralph Barnes, Dick Becker, Don Bowles, Tom Cantrill, Tom Dunning, George DuPont, Jim Hradecky, Don Keithley, Stew Leonard, Sr., Stew Leonard, Jr., Graham Morris, Dave Power, Liener Temerlin, Lee Wilkins.

The following are the people who make our company successful. I hope I can be worthy of their trust.

SEWELL BUICK-HYUNDAI: Joe Alexander, Aubrey Austin, Brenna Beddingfield, Ryan Bevington, Charles Breedlove, Larry Buie, Victor Burns, Ann Butsch, Richard Butsch, Scott Chadwick, L. C. Chatham, Ganeen Colgrove, John Condron, Bettye Cromeans, Gary Cromeans, Mark Daniels, Diane Doggett, Ted Dooley, Jim Echols, Tammy Edney, Cheryl Elliott, Cedric Farmer, Tony Froning, Milton Galbreath, Jimmy Gilbert, Lynette Green, Paul Harding, Rick Hawksley, Kevin Howe, Mary Howe, Glaze Hutchins, Vance Jackman, Mark Jenkins, Carrie Johnson, Terry Johnson, Kathy Jondle, Sharon Keuper, Eddie Krause, Gary Lacy, Keith Martin, John Massey, Dave Mataczynski, Melissa McClure, Tony Morales, Casey Moreland, Louise Moreland, Tamara Neef, Gary Nichols, Jack Ollie, Donna Parks, Jim Paulk, Bret Poteet, Rodney Richmond, Tony Robertson, Tom Rush, Carl Sandberg, Mark Schulz, Mickey Seiler, Wes Sisk, David Sivils, Alan Sperry, Greg Stovall, Shawn Strange, Suzie Tittle, Lonnie Usery, Mel Warren, Clarence Washington, Dan Weiss, Drew Wight.

SEWELL CADILLAC-CHEVROLET: Pat Alonzo, Willie Barnes, Mark Baudean, Donald Bealer, Joe Raymond Berniard, Larry Bieser, Sarah Blair, Darren Blanchard, Clarence Boone, Patti Bordelon, Smokey Briggs, Miles Caire, Frank Caruso, Jr., Donald Coffelt, Jr., Al Collins, Sam Cormick, Bill Cristina, Jim Davies, Otis Delatte, Wendel Delatte, David Diaz, David Diket, Bill Dunbar, Eric Eilers, Morris Flores, James Foucha, Jr., Eddie Gabriel, Butch Gautier, Archie Gipson, Tom Guercio, David Guess, Jamie Guidry, Eddie Guillot, Gordon Hanna, Leona Harris, Stephanie Held, Alex Hoffman, David Hoover, Jennifer Hornyak, Charley Howley, Larry Hurd, Joshua Johnson, Charlie Jones, Dawna Jones, Michael Jung, Paul Kimble, Tequilla Lation, S. J. Ledet, Steve Lopez, Edward Lott, Mike Mast, Joe Matherne, Ed McCarthy, Jim McGrew, Lewin McNab, Terry McNeal, Scott Michel, Rhonda Montegut, Judy Morrow, Mark Odom, Timothy Palazzotto, Christopher Pattison, Joseph Pepitone, Lucius Perron, Raymel Porché, Jane Price, Linda Reed, Wayne Richard, Tammy Rodrigue, Mickey Roye, Claud Ruffin, Frank Russo, John Russo, Janis Shreve, Joe Sims, Marvin Smith, Patrick Smith, Tom Starnes, Doug Stead, Deloris Stiles, Carol Strunk, Stan Stuart, Mike Symms, George Torres, Leonard Travis, John Triplett, James Warner, Dorothy Wiggins, William Willkomm.

SEWELL LEXUS: Tommy Armstrong, Tom Batson, Dee Butler, Judy Conley, Tim Darling, Bobby Dawson, Albert Diaz, Phoebe Franco, Dan Frogge, John Godyn, Jim Goodsell, Mary Grether, Steve Holloway, Bruce Hood, Judy Hummel, Elbert Hutchins, Gerald Jackson, Curt Jenkins, Dave Johnson, Greg Johnson, Jo Lacy, Stephan Lauson, David Leffall, Blane Mathis, Cecily McClarin, Bill McKinney, Hoyte Palmer, Bob Perry, Barry Pryor, Aldo Ramirez, R. J. Reynolds, Maritza Richard, Leroy Rush, Steve Salik, Rob Schweizer, Rusty Scruby, Dan Sedelic, Steve Simmons, Mark Smith, Keith Spring, Charisse Stinson, James Thompson, Kelly Vickers, Aaron Windes.

SEWELL OLDSMOBILE: Steve Alsbrook, Tony Ballard, Herman Barge, Willie Cantu, Lee Craig, Richard Creighton, Donald Crum, Jon Davenport, Elijah Dawson, Edd Deen, John Densmore, Mark Downey, Brian Dunne, Bob Eckert, Marcelino Espinosa, Daryl Ewry, James Freel, Robert Fry, Steve Fuentes, Garven Garcia, Leonard Garza, Rita Gibbs, Guy Gimenez, Juan Gomez, Arnulfo Gutierrez, Tim Hall, Earl Holcombe, Grover Holder, Joe Johnson, Tim Jones, Fred Katani, Bill Kausch, Joe Koubek, Daryl Kvapil, Renee Landrum, Bernie Maag, Stan Maxwell, Mike Melton, Peggy Miller, Keith Morris, Cecil Pettijohn, Bubba Prewitt, Julie Ramsden, Bob Rayburn, Billy Richardson, Fred Roberts, Kay Schlattweiler, Brent Sharpley, Bob Skrivanek, Larry Smith, Mark Smith, Ismael Soto, Karl Stefankiewicz, Mark Stovall, Carolyn Taylor, Ronnie Thompson, Kelley Todd, Joyce Vantreese, Michael Ward.

SEWELL VILLAGE CADILLAC/STERLING: Charles Abbott, Jeff Allbritten, Chris Allen, Freddy Alvarado, Murray Arbuckle, Serjio Arreola, Dennis Askew, Gary Ault, Juan Ayala, Scott Bachman, Dan Bailey, Dick Baker, Don Bane, Rock Barker, Wiley Barker, Al Barnard, Vanessa Barnett, Robert Barrera, Joy Bastian, Forrest Battle, Greg Baxter, Sarge Beilharz, Billy Joe Bell, Chuck Bellows, Marcus Bills, Jim Bird, Floyd Black, Marc Blades, James Boney, Robert Bradshaw, Lee Braly, Danny Branum, Al Brentlinger, James Brigdon, Lisa Brion, Tony Brown, Duward Burgess, Ed Calbridge, Jack Campbell, Bob Carpenter, Joe Carroll, James Cartridge, Jordan Case, Calvin Choice, Mike Clark, Doyle Clifton, Rich Clonts, Johnny Colbert, Terri Colley, Rick Cowart, Steven Crandall, Curley Crawford, Ron Crawford, Cheri Crow, Harvey Crowley, Alma Cuellar, Mark Culbert, Beth Cunningham, Kevin Danheiser, Keith Daniels, Craig Davenport, Jeff Davis, Rod Davis, Dennis Decet, Clarence Diggs, Joe Diggs, Rick Dralle, Mark Dunbar, Phil Dunnet, Glenn Dzioba, Bob Edwards, Ron Everett, Adolph Farfan, Robert Filosof, A. F. Flentroy, Bruce Foster, Margaret Franklin, Shellie Galloway, Bryan Galt, Juan Garcia, Dan Garner, Jim Gibbs, Chris Gilliland, Craig Given, James Goldenberg, Alan Goss, David Gossett, Eric Green, Richard Greene, Jerry Griffin, Othella Gumm, Gus Gustafson, Manuel Gutierrez, Doug Hale, Gene Hale, James Hall, Mike Hammar, Pete Harding, Jeff Hargrove, Benny Harris, Sandy Harwood, Frank Head, Lynn Heath, John Heuss, Richard Hitzfield, Vic Hitzfield, William Hix, Grover Holder, Barbara Hollenbeck, Mike Hooper, Sandy Howard, John Huff, Willie Hutchins, Tim Ihrig, Yvonne Jackson, Delores Jefferson, Jimi Johns, Daren Johnson, David Johnson, Lou Johnson, Frankie Jones, Phil Jones, Phil Jordan, Scott Kapes, Jill Keim, Gene Keith, Cindy Kell, Billy Kinney, Norris Kinney, Steve Kittelson, George Klongland, Billy Kuntz, Pat Kuntz, Roger Lackey, Jack Lacy, Ed Landwehr, George Langlais, Ruben Lara, Paul Latham, Mike Lawrence, Young Lee, Mike Lees, Jack Lewis, T. J. Lider, Annie Lightfoot, Jack Lilley, Ernie Longchamp, Darrell Luna, Corey Maples, Marthann March, Jim Martin, Kimberlee Martin, Starla Martin, Jose Martinez, Juan Martinez, Nelson Masi, Conrad Masterson, Pat Maxfield, Hank Mazinski, Don McCants, Daniel McClure, Burke McDavid, Boyne McHargue, Eric McHenry, Harvey McHenry, Don McLaurin, Thomas McTurner, Brent Melton, Mary Moreland, Rusty Moreland, Randy Morrison, Lynn Nitcher, James Novy, Frank Oldfield, Les Oliver, Greg Olson, Neva Owens, Jimmy Pang, Nam Soo Park, Henry Parker, Rich Parker, Paul Patterson, Rickey Peoples, Glen Peters, Melissa Petzold, Kelvin Pleasant, Kyle Pliskal, Shorty Ponce, Brenda Prewitt, Frank Pritzen, Mike Proctor, Julian Quezada, Mary Ransom, Fina Reid, Mario Retta, Bill Richburg, Jim Ringholm, Mike Roe, Cathy Roeder, Charles Rogers, Tiody Rojo, Barry Rubin, Sonny Ruff, Joe Ruiz, Jeff Sabold, Tony Sanchez, Joel Saripalli, Steve Schaffer, Johnny Schoonover, Carole Seidel, Danny Seitzler, Louise Sewell, Chris

Shaffer, Tommy Shaffer, Cary Simmons, Rhonda Singer, Red Sledge, Ray Smallwood, Mike Smith, Steven Solaja, Cathy Sorrell, Darlene Stark, Mickey Stewart, Ronnie Stewart, Jeff Summers, Frank Tanner, Mona Taylor, Susan Taylor-Kell, David Thomas, Frank Thompson, Lee Thompson, Debbie Toler, Tommy Toney, Frankie Torres, Jesse Torres, Jesse Trevino, Dan Turk, Erin Urias, Carl Velasquez, Linda Vick, Mike Vogt, Carl Wachholz, Mike Waitkus, Rita Walker, Van Walker, Billy Watkins, Wayne Weehunt, David Weimer, Jack Whillock, Charles Whitlow, Jackie Wilburn, David Wildman, George Wiley, Bob Williams, David Williams, Farrell Williams, Glen Williams, Dawn Williamson, John Willis, Betty Wilson, Charlie Wilson, Trudy Wolf, Jim Wood, Lee Woodall, Gary Wright, Seung Yi, Merle Zachary, Ron Zohfeld, Artur Zwolski.

The people at the Goldhirsh Group should be singled out for their patience. Thanks to Bernie Goldhirsh, Joel Novack, and (yes, even) Mark Reisch.

Since it must seem to the people at *Inc.* that they have been hearing about this project since 1953, it only seems fair to acknowledge their good nature, suggestions, and aid. To George Gendron, Michael Hopkins, Nancy Lyons, Jeffrey Seglin, and Sara Noble, just remember this: no good deed ever goes unpunished.

We have to single out Elaine M. Cummings and Jane Yee. Not only did Elaine transcribe countless hours of tapes, she highlighted areas she thought we should expand upon. Her instincts were never wrong. Jane managed to keep the printer running through endless revisions, and she never once complained.

Barbara Rudolph made sure the tone remained consistent and Debbie Orenstein and Rick Pappas did the impossible—they gave lawyers a good name.

And we owe a special thanks to Harriet Rubin, executive editor at Doubleday, who without ever once donning cowboy (girl, Harriet?) boots made this book far better than we ever thought possible.

Janet Coleman is officially nominated for sainthood, for seeing this project through.

Anne Christine Peck, Peter James Peck Brown, and Shannon Rachel Peck Brown put up with early morning phone calls, late night calls, and endless meetings and plane trips in between. This was far harder on them than it was on us. Thanks, guys.

And finally a personal note from Carl Sewell: Paul Brown wrote this book. He spent hour after hour—over a two-year period—listening, organizing, translating, and clarifying what I was trying to describe. I have the utmost respect for his ability and his professionalism. He arrived as "the writer." He will remain as a friend.

Ross Puskar and his team at Puskar, Gibbon and Chapin deserve a special thanks. Ross spent more hours than he would care to count helping with everything from what the cover could look like to the focus groups conducted by Yankelovich, Skelly and White/Clancy, Shulman. His advice and counsel were always appreciated.

Alen Hollomon is responsible for the design of our buildings. He has combined form, function, and durability. For his perspective and his work, we are deeply indebted to him.

John Sewell died of lung cancer May 5, 1990. He was my cousin, my teacher, my partner, and my friend. We all learned so much from him and will miss him for the rest of our lives.

Most of all, I need to thank my family, who have lived with my passion for the automobile business and now have endured the writing of this book. I love them more than they know.